Struggle and Suffrage in Halifax

Struggle and Suffrage in Halifax

Women's Lives and the Fight for Equality

Helena Fairfax

PEN & SWORD
HISTORY

AN IMPRINT OF PEN & SWORD BOOKS LTD.
YORKSHIRE – PHILADELPHIA

First published in Great Britain in 2019
Pen & Sword HISTORY
An imprint of Pen & Sword Books Ltd
Yorkshire – Philadelphia

Copyright © Helena Fairfax, 2019
ISBN: 978 1 52671 777 1

A CIP catalogue record for this book is available from the British Library

Printed and bound in the UK by TJ International, Padstow, Cornwall

Pen & Sword Books Limited incorporates the imprints of Atlas, Archaeology,
Aviation, Discovery, Family History, Fiction, History, Maritime, Military, Military
Classics, Politics, Select, Transport, True Crime, Air World, Frontline Publishing, Leo
Cooper, Remember When, Seaforth Publishing, The Praetorian Press, Wharncliffe
Local History, Wharncliffe Transport, Wharncliffe True Crime and White Owl.

For a complete list of Pen & Sword titles please contact
PEN & SWORD BOOKS LIMITED
47 Church Street, Barnsley, South Yorkshire, S70 2AS, England
E-mail: enquiries@pen-and-sword.co.uk • Website: www.pen-and-sword.co.uk
Or
PEN AND SWORD BOOKS
1950 Lawrence Rd, Havertown, PA 19083, USA
E-mail: Uspen-and-sword@casematepublishers.com
Website: www.penandswordbooks.com

Contents

Introduction   vii

Acknowledgements   x

Chapter One: Child Labour and Girls at Work   **1**
  Girls at Work in the Card-Making Industry   1
  Girls at Work in the Textile Mills   6
  Girls at Work in the Mines   17

Chapter Two: An Unequal Education   **25**
  The Early Years   25
  'A cruel injustice.' The Schools Inquiry Commission
  1867-68   32
  The Focus on Domestic Science   41
  Further Education: the Halifax girls 'not burdened
  with a serious education'   46

Chapter Three: Women's Health and Domestic Lives   **51**
  Women's Chores in the Home   51
  Courtship and Marriage   59
  Sexual Abuse and Harassment   65
  Pregnancy and Childbirth   71
  Birth Control   77

Chapter Four: Women in Employment   **89**
  What Did Middle-Class Women Do?   89
  Working-Class Women and Their Jobs   99
  Women in Domestic Service   102
  Women at Work in the Mills, Factories and Engineering   110
  The Halifax Building Society: 'No Female Shall Be
  Admitted to Any Office Therein'   129

Chapter Five: Chartism, Radical Politics, and Votes for Women   **139**

Halifax Women and Nineteenth Century Radical Politics   139

The Halifax Suffragettes   149

Halifax Suffragettes and the Boycott of the 1911 Census   171

Bibliography   175

Citations   183

Index   195

Introduction

'A Toast to the Ladies'

Women's fight for equality from 1800–1950 meant far more than the fight for the vote, important though that victory is. Their struggle covered almost every area of their lives.

I'm not a historian. I write fiction, and in my stories women take centre stage. In the twenty-first century romance novel, the heroine's independence is taken for granted. She has her own money, she has her own interests and friends, she's not looking for a man to look after her and make her life complete. Before starting out on this book, I wrote about women who were firmly at the centre of their own stories. Writing a history of women's lives in Halifax was a step outside my normal sphere, but I accepted it as a challenge. And as for researching women's lives, really, how hard could that be? I looked forward to discovering much from the wealth of information I expected to find in the archives.

And this is some of what I discovered: in 1837, a board of thirty-one men oversaw the operation of Halifax's workhouses; Edward Akroyd, the millionaire textile manufacturer, was the founder of the first Working Men's College outside London; Halifax Town Hall was designed by Charles Barry, who designed the Houses of Parliament; the People's Park was donated by wealthy industrialist Sir Francis Crossley, 'so that every working man in Halifax … shall go to take his stroll there after he has done his hard day's toil.'

And so it went on. As I leafed through the history books, I began to wonder whether Halifax was entirely populated by men in the nineteenth century. Where on earth had fifty per cent of the population disappeared to? While the men were strolling through the park at the end of their working day, what were the women doing? I pictured them at home, still hard at work after their own 'hard day's toil' in the factory, scrubbing floors and mending clothes and feeding the children. I felt them as a completely silent presence, unrecorded in the archives, their mouths bound.

I found a report in a newspaper which I read several times over. On 14 January 1839, a dinner was held at the Oddfellows' Hall in honour of Mr Peter Bussey, a Chartist and agitator for 'universal suffrage'. In those days only the wealthy could vote (and only wealthy men, at that). The Chartists were fighting for the vote to be extended to all men, regardless of income. It was a noble cause, but the terminology still jars, almost 200 years later. How could 'universal suffrage' be universal, if it didn't include women?

The evening began with a toast to 'The People – the only source of legitimate power'. This is the part I read several times, in order to make sure I fully understood. It's a worthy toast, but since the dinner ended with a toast to 'The Ladies', I could only draw the conclusion that 'The Ladies' were evidently not considered of 'The People'. In the final irony, 'The Ladies' were not even given the opportunity to answer their own toast. It was responded to 'in an enthusiastic speech by Mr G. J. Harney of London, who was applauded most warmly'.

Well done, Mr Harney. There isn't a single mention of a woman in the entire article, and yet they must have been there. Were they just ghostly figures, shimmering in their evening finery, their mouths opening in vain, unable to make themselves heard?

Researching this book, I began to discover for myself what Virginia Woolf described so aptly in her essay on 'Women and Fiction' in 1929. The answer to the history of women's lives, 'lies locked in old diaries, stuffed away in old drawers, half-obliterated in the memories of the aged. It is to be found in the lives of the obscure... For very little is known about women.

The history of England is the history of the male line, not of the female.'

By peering through the cracks of established sources, and by closing the history books and looking instead for 'old diaries', memoirs and letters, I have gradually been piecing together a picture of the lives of the women of Halifax. Researching this book has been an eye-opener. It has made me realise just how far women have come on the road to equality, how far there still is to go, and just how easily everything could be lost. It has made me think far more deeply about the countries where women's voices are still not heard today, and about the shame of so many women being invisible and unacknowledged in the history books.

This book is just a tiny snapshot of some of the key events in women's lives in Halifax from 1800–1950. It is a small 'Toast to the Ladies'; to all those bright, hard-working, tough, spirited women who once lived in Halifax, and who contributed unsung to the greater good of theirs and our society.

Acknowledgements

I'd like to thank the following for their generous help and support: Warner Baxter, John Saville, and the staff of Calderdale Industrial Museum; Amy Binns and Douglas Simpson; Malcolm Bull for his invaluable website; Philip Cockcroft; John Critchley; Steve Gee for his very generous donation of photos; David Glover and Mike Brook of the Halifax Antiquarian Society; Ann Kilbey and the staff of the Pennine Horizons Digital Archive; John Uttley; Nicholas Walker; Sian Yates of Lloyds Banking Group Archives; the members of the Old Photos of Halifax Group on FB; the staff of Calderdale and Huddersfield Libraries; the staff of the West Yorkshire Archive Services in Wakefield and Halifax.

CHAPTER ONE

Child Labour and Girls at Work

Girls at Work in the Card-Making Industry

The growth of the town of Halifax might never have happened without the labour of small girls and boys. This is a deeply uncomfortable realisation for us in the twenty-first century, but for earlier generations it was considered acceptable for working-class children to work – and even desirable.

In the 1720s, Daniel Defoe admired the way children in the hills around Halifax were kept, 'busy carding, spinning', and how, 'hardly anything above four years old, but its hands are not sufficient to itself'.[1]

Defoe was an educated, middle-class man, born in the noisy streets of Cripplegate in London. As he journeyed through the Calder Valley, the sight of so many women and children at work in this spectacular setting seemed to him idyllic. But if Defoe had stopped long enough to talk to the 4-year-old girls at their toil, what would they have told him?

A hundred years after Defoe's visit, at the beginning of the nineteenth century, much of the cottage industry around Halifax had declined. One process, though, continued to be carried out by hand long after others were mechanised. Thousands of women and children in Halifax and surroundings were employed as card-setters. Their work was vital to the textile industry.

Carding is the process of passing wool fibres through 'cards' clothed with thin metal teeth. It's a dirty business in which the muck from the sheep's wool is removed before the fibres are

Woman carding. Etching by Jean François Millet 1855. Original at Brooklyn Museum, NY

sent for spinning. The women and children Defoe passed in the hills would have been carding the wool by hand, using cards shaped like square bats. In 1775, Richard Arkwright patented a new carding machine – mechanised rollers covered in leather and wire teeth. After this, and with the rapid expansion of the textile industry, there was an explosion in the amount of card clothing (the leather and teeth) required for his machines, and all of this had to be assembled by hand.

Cutting the leather to fit the rollers was a job done mainly by men. Several card-making businesses in Halifax are listed in White's Directory of 1837. John Drake, of 28 Woolshops, for example, or George Horsfall, of 29 Pellon Lane, or John Holdsworth, of South Parade. The men would cut out rectangles of leather and punch regular rows of thousands of holes in the strips, using a contraption called a 'Tommy Pricker' or 'stang'. They would then 'draw', or stretch, lengths of metal by battering wire coils on a stone flag. The lengths would be cut and bent into individual teeth.

Setting the metal teeth into the leather was a job done almost entirely by women and children. The men would load the leather and teeth in saddlebags and distribute them around the countryside on horseback, travelling up into the dwellings on the hillsides which Defoe had passed through a hundred years previously. With so much material to distribute – and with the threat of robbery of the vast amount of wages involved – the men often used agents to do this work for them.

The women and children were paid by the piece and for accuracy. There is very little record left of these thousands of workers. Early censuses recorded only the occupation of the head of the household, who was nearly always male. In the 1930s, Selwyn Walker wrote a history of Joseph Sykes Brothers, his family's card-clothing business in Lindley, Huddersfield. Walker's history provides rare and fascinating anecdotal evidence of how the women and children toiled at home all day, bent over the leather, not stopping even as night fell. The women would huddle around a candle, singing rhymes to help the tiny children keep count and keep up their speed:

'There's one for me, one for Sam, and ahr Mary, ahr
Tom and ahr John, for Mrs Naylor t'next door, and
their Sal and Betty and old Ben',

and so on until the whole village had been included, even to the
parson and his dog.[2]

As the children grew older, the boys moved on to other
occupations, but the girls continued to work at home, and by the
time they were grown women they could set teeth with a nimbleness
and accuracy which must have been astonishing to witness.

Besides employing women and children in their own homes,
many card-making businesses also employed orphans from
the workhouse. 'Setting schools' were established in the card-
makers' premises in Halifax, where children sat in great rows,
stooped over their work. Their time was regimented. Forced to
sit, day after day, for hours on end, they frequently developed
health problems such as curvature of the spine. One little card-
setter, 'at the age of 4 years, sat with other children on little low
forms, setting the teeth into the leather by hand. She told how
the children cried when they pricked their fingers and how cross
the master was when any blood got onto the cards.'[3]

The men running the businesses paid their women and
children outworkers very little. When they supplied materials to
other card-makers, however, they insisted on being paid a decent
rate. In 1833, the Halifax card-clothing manufacturers formed
a secret society, meeting at the Lord Nelson Inn in Luddenden
and the Whitehall Hotel, Hipperholme. Members of the society
included James Keighley, of 13 Broad St, and John Whitely,
of 5 Winding Rd. They sent several letters to Joseph Sykes
demanding higher rates for the leather and teeth they were
supplying. For pricking (punching) the men demanded 14*d* per
dozen yards of punched leather. Using the 'stang', as many as
480 holes could be punched in one go. By contrast, they paid
the women and children card-setters as little as a half-penny per
1,400 teeth set by hand.[4]

After 200 years, and with no records existing from the
women, we can only speculate on the reasons why they didn't

group together in the same way to demand better pay. One reason almost certainly is that the men had better means to organise themselves. Crucially, they were able to write and could communicate by letter. They owned horses and could travel to meetings. They met in pubs, which 'respectable' women rarely entered in those days. The only place the women could have gathered was in their own homes – homes owned by their husbands or fathers, who may not have condoned a protest. Piecework was irregular, and the women may have been so grateful to be offered the work at all, they would accept it on low terms. The fact that children and orphans also laboured as teeth-setters meant there was a constant supply of cheap labour, and holding out for higher payment could mean families being passed over and the work simply given to the next needy family.

At its peak in the 1830s, card-making gave employment to as many as 20,000 women and children in the Parish of Halifax,

Cotton carding machine 1858

which stretched in those days from Rishworth to Wadsworth. This is an astonishing figure and was almost a fifth of the total population. The industry collapsed almost overnight, with what must have been catastrophic results for the women and families involved.

In 1839, an inventor called James Walton launched a card-clothing machine that revolutionised the process of teeth-setting, making production faster and cheaper. Machine manufacturers were quick to start producing it. In the 1840s, Joseph Sykes Brothers, who had given card-setting piecework to many families, began dealings with Thomas Crabtree, card-setting machine makers in Halifax. The Official Catalogue of the Great Exhibition of 1851 lists on display, 'A card-setting machine for producing the complete card, from the wire and leather, or cloth.' Walter Sykes records that it was 'a very wonderful and intricate contrivance in those days'.[6]

The machine was quickly adopted in the mills in Halifax. The men who had previously organised the cottage industry were able to take up jobs operating the new machines, but for the women and children, card-setting and the income derived from it disappeared almost overnight. Many families were forced to leave their homes in the hills and come to Halifax to find work, adding to the troubles of a crowded and insanitary town.

Girls at Work in the Textile Mills

On 16 October 1830, the *Leeds Mercury* printed a typical selection of readers' letters. One reader described the paintings he'd seen at a recent exhibition, with their 'romantic airy forms … and superior taste'. One had written in with a poem, in flowery nineteenth-century verse, extolling 'The British Oak', with acorns, 'graceful to the sight', and, 'mistletoe, and berries white'.

These were the sort of gentle, innocuous letters the *Mercury*'s middle-class, conservative readers liked to peruse over their breakfast. But on the same day, slap-bang in the middle of these items, and all the more shocking in contrast, the *Mercury* also printed one of the most incendiary letters ever to appear in a Yorkshire newspaper. The letter was entitled 'Slavery in Yorkshire', it was written by Richard Oastler, and its wording still has the power to shock today:

> Scenes of misery, acts of oppression, and victims of slavery, even on the threshold of our homes! ... thousands of little children, both male and female, but principally female ... daily compelled to labour from six o'clock in the morning to seven in the evening ... compelled, not by the cart-whip of the negro slave-driver, but by the dread of the equally appalling thong

A girl crawls under a loom in Frances Trollope's The Life and Adventures of Michael Armstrong *(Illustration by Auguste Hervieu 1876)*

of the overlooker, to hasten, half-dressed, but not half-
fed, to those magazines of British Infantile Slavery!

Yorkshire mill owners were being compared to slave drivers.
Sitting at their comfortable breakfasts, James Akroyd and the
other manufacturers of Halifax must have choked on their
morning tea.

News of Oastler's letter quickly reached the mill workers
themselves. One later remembered, 'I was then a factory girl
working 14 hours a day, and tired as I was when my father was
reading it, my heart was lifted up to think that somebody felt
for us.'[7]

The letter provoked an angry response from mill owners.
Simeon Townend, a mill owner from Thornton, claimed, 'little
girls were necessary for the spinning machines, because they
were quick and clean in their work. Moreover, though their day
was long their work was "far from laborious".'[8]

What sort of work, done by infant girls, was so 'necessary'?
The youngest children would usually be employed as 'scavengers',
sweeping up the waste. Adults were too large to crawl under the
looms and spinning machines, and even children had to make
themselves as small as possible as the machines rattled and
clattered at tremendous speed above their heads. They would
be given a small brush; losing the brush could mean a fine or a
beating, and many of them tied the brushes round their wrists
with a leather strap for safe-keeping. This meant they risked
not just a scalping, but having an arm crushed if the brush got
caught.

Children employed as 'doffers' changed the bobbins (doffs)
on the spinning machines. When the bobbins were full, the
machinery stopped. A whistle would blow and the doffers would
race onto the frames. Machine downtime meant lost money,
and any doffers who didn't replace a bobbin quickly enough
risked a beating.

It was the girls employed as 'piecers' that Townsend claimed
were 'necessary'. Piecers worked for the spinners, who controlled
between seventy to a hundred spindles. It was the piecer's job to

repair any threads that broke during the spinning process. With so many spindles to look after, the job required concentration and dexterity, as well as the stamina to stand and walk up and down for hours on end.

One spinner said,

> I find it difficult to keep my piecers awake the last hour of a winter's evening; have seen them fall asleep, and go on performing their work with their hands while they were asleep, after the billey [spinning machine] had stopped, when their work was over; I have stopped and looked at them for two minutes, going through the motions of piecening when they were fast asleep, when there was no work to do, and they were doing nothing.[9]

John Fielden was a factory reformer who owned a cotton mill in Todmorden. In a speech to the House of Commons on 9 May 1836, he stated:

> At a meeting in Manchester a man claimed that a child in one mill walked twenty-four miles a day. I was surprised by this statement, therefore … I went into my own factory, and with a clock before me, I watched a child at work, and having watched her for some time, I then calculated the distance she had to go in a day, and to my surprise, I found it nothing short of twenty miles.

The children's working day could start as early as 6 a.m. Anyone arriving late risked being 'quartered', that is, having a quarter of the day's pay docked. Children and their parents were terrified of oversleeping. Many paid a penny a week to a 'knocker-up' who would go round the streets banging on doors, making sure everyone was awake.

The masters in Halifax were said to be among the worst offenders regarding children's working conditions. They were also the most intransigent when it came to reform. On 5 March 1831, five months after Oastler's letter was published, James Akroyd chaired a meeting of factory owners in the upstairs room

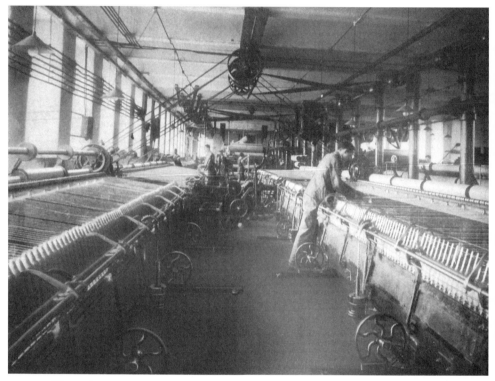

Worsted spinning mules, Crossley's Carpets E mill (Company Brochure 1926)

at the Old Cock Inn, Halifax, along with representatives of the Rawson, Holdsworth and Crossley families, and others. These hard, commercial men, in their dark suits, ranged themselves around a long table by the warmth of the fire, their beer and coffee in front of them, to discuss the conditions of the girls and boys who worked for them.

A clerk was there to take the minutes. The mill masters concluded: 'That the character of the generality of master worsted spinners in respect to humanity, kindness, and considerate attention to those in their employ is unimpeachable.'[10]

Oastler was quick to express his disgust: '"Is it possible," he asked, "that avarice and self-interest can have such a bewildering effect on the mind of man?"'[11]

Faced with such obduracy, Oastler and his supporters had a long and difficult struggle ahead, despite the support among working people. On 6 March 1832, almost exactly a year after the meeting at the Old Cock, still nothing had changed. Vast crowds turned out in high winds and rain in Halifax to hear Oastler speak:

> The other morning two little girls came to a mill in this town just five minutes past six. The morning was dark, cold and wet. They had a mile and a half to walk and were wet through. They were shut out of the mill and refused entrance. They turned towards a boiler house, intending to dry their clothes. There also they were rejected, and the poor creatures had to seek a place of shelter, which they found about half a mile off, where they were allowed to dry and warm themselves. At nine they returned to the mill and had half a day's wages taken off for being five minutes late... The crowd began to shout, 'Akroyd, Akroyd! Shame, shame!'[12]

Ten days after Oastler's open air meeting in Halifax, MP Michael Sadler spoke to the House of Commons, proposing a reduction in the hours of work for all people under 18 to ten a day. The House agreed there should be an enquiry into child labour, which Sadler headed. Over the next few months, Sadler and his colleagues interviewed workers, doctors and bystanders in mills and factories about the effects of their working conditions on children. Sadler's findings include witness statements such as this, from Samuel Coulson, the father of three daughters aged 8, 11 and 12:

> We had to take [the girls] up asleep and shake them ... before we could get them off to their work ... my mistress used to stop up all night, for fear that we could not get them ready for the time: sometimes we have gone to bed, and one of us generally woke up ... we have cried often when we have given them the little victualling we had to give them; we had to shake them, and they have fallen to sleep with the victuals in their mouths many a time.[13]

Sadler's report was published in 1833, to another outcry. Even then, parliament was slow to act. Many maintained Sadler's choice of witnesses and method of questioning were unbalanced. Another Royal Commission followed. This time those questioned were obliged to answer under oath.

John Holdsworth, of Shaw Lodge Mills, was one of the mill owners questioned. When asked the age of the youngest in his employ, and whether she had previously worked elsewhere, he replied, 'Seven years old is the youngest; only one at that age. They cannot have been employed at any other trades, unless card-setting, of which we are not certain.'[14]

When asked, Holdsworth told the commissioners that corporal punishment was not allowed in his establishment and that he had never been informed of any instance of its infliction on the children in his employ.

James Akroyd had recently opened his imposing Old Lane Mill in Northowram. When asked the same question, he replied, 'Hands from nine to fifteen years of age are most liable to want correction. I consider it would be totally impossible to do without correction where so many children come together.'[15] 'Correction' was a euphemism for a beating.

In 1833, factory reformer George Crabtree took a tour around the mills in the Calder Valley. In a long letter to Richard Oastler he describes his visits, including a visit to 11-year-old Mary Holland. Mary's mother was a widow with six children, and Mary was sick at home:

> Her illness was occasioned by overworking, she had been ill six weeks, she works from six to eight, and very little time allowed for meals... The spinner has a stick to beat them with, and sometimes beats her with a Billy-Roller and raises great lumps on her head, she says they break their heads at Rawson's factory ... they stop their wages for going late or doing anything wrong.[16]

Crabtree also called on mill owner Mr Greenup in Sowerby Bridge. He was told by the woman who opened the door that,

James Akroyd's imposing Old Mill, now derelict

'she was sure all their children were very comfortable'. As he passed Greenup's mill, however, he heard a scream:

> On looking round, we saw an elder sister holding the hand of a younger in her pinafore, and running home. When we inquired into the affair, she had got her fingers entangled in the machinery, and they were all torn off: – Well, thought I, so much for Mrs. Greenup's comfortable work people.[17]

The factory campaign in Yorkshire was run by men. By comparison, in 1834 in the United States, women workers at Lowell Textile Mills in Massachusetts were striking for better pay. These same women subsequently banded together to campaign for the introduction of the Ten Hour Bill in America.

Where were the women of Halifax in the factory campaigns? In his letter to Oastler, Crabtree wrote: 'Mothers of Halifax and its neighbourhood, rouse yourselves in your children's cause; if the RICH ladies won't use their influence to emancipate your infants, you as mothers ought to be alive to the amelioration of their condition.'[18]

From our modern perspective it's hard for most of us to imagine the exhaustion and fear caused by grinding poverty. Many mothers in Halifax worked to the point of collapse and had little time or energy left for organising themselves in protest. They also faced the very real fear of losing their jobs if they agitated for better conditions. Michael Sadler discovered that at least six of the workers he'd spoken to had later been sacked for giving evidence to the parliamentary committee. America was then a relatively new country for the European women who had emigrated there, and it's possible the striking women of Massachusetts simply had more confidence that their voices would be heard. We shouldn't underestimate the lack of confidence among working-class women in Halifax at that time. After centuries of being made to feel their political opinions – and those of their menfolk – were valueless, they may well have felt convinced no one would listen.

It's difficult to know just how much influence even Crabtree's 'rich ladies' of Halifax could have had over the way mill owners such as Akroyd decided to run their businesses. Women at the time had no voice in government, and it would have been completely unacceptable for a middle-class woman to speak out in a public forum or have a say in manufacturing. Her place was in the home. The middle-class women of Halifax raised vast sums of money for charity, as will be seen in a later chapter. They also exerted what influence they could in causes regarded as socially acceptable, such as the Anti-Corn Law League. The Corn Laws of 1815 had artificially increased the price of corn, which benefited aristocratic landowners. Middle-class manufacturers such as Crossley and Akroyd wanted repeal of the Corn Laws because they believed it would lead to free trade for their goods. (The fact that the Corn Laws inflated the price of bread, which affected the poor, was a secondary concern.)

On 30 November 1842, the women of Halifax organised a great Anti-Corn Law Demonstration in the form of a tea party, held at the Oddfellows' Hall. They decorated the room 'in scarlet and white merino', and the affair was attended by Crossley, Akroyd, and many other influential men of Halifax. Although the women did all the organising, they were certainly not expected to speak. There is evidence from this meeting, though, that Halifax women did visit working people, even if they didn't support Oastler's campaign. Mr Morris, who chaired the meeting, spoke of the women's many, 'visits of charity to the houses of the labouring population, [where] they saw many sad evidences of suffering and privation.'[19]

Halifax was a small town in 1830, with a population of less than 20,000. The middle classes moved in a small social sphere, dominated by a few families. For middle-class women to agitate for the Anti-Corn Law league was both fashionable and socially acceptable, but to speak out in support of working-class children and against the employment practices of the manufacturers of the town would have been unthinkable.

Women of the working-classes also had little opportunity to have their voice heard in public, but Oastler had enormous support among them. In April 1832, he organised a 'Pilgrimage of Mercy' to York. At least 12,000 people marched miles from across Yorkshire to hear him. Women's presence at this enormous gathering has always been underplayed. One newspaper report stated that, 'many parties of operatives entered the city very early… A continuance of rain, however, unfortunately rendered the *poor men* very uncomfortable.'[20] (My emphasis.)

Another Yorkshire newspaper reported, 'Besides the mere procession (and it amounted to many thousand *men*) an immense number of *persons* moved along with it…'[21] (My emphasis.)

Who were these 'persons' in the procession? Cecil Driver, in his biography of Oastler, wrote that, 'in some districts even the women suddenly caught the thrill and joined the procession too.'[22]

Driver's account surely completely underestimates the women's motives for attending the march – and is even patronising. Women outnumbered men in the mills. By all accounts the weather on the day of the procession was atrocious. It's extremely unlikely that working women, already worn out from hours at work, would have considered an exhausting walk for miles in a downpour a 'thrill'.

T. W. Hanson published *The Story of Old Halifax* in 1920; he would have been able to interview people whose parents or grandparents had eyewitness accounts of the march. Hanson writes, 'Men, *women, and children* walked from all parts of the West Riding … York Racecourse was crowded with the multitude of people, many of whom suffered greatly by their long march to York and home again in bad weather.'[23] (My emphasis.)

In 1833, a year after Oastler's march, a Factory Act was passed making it an offence to employ a child under 9 years of age. Children under 13 were limited to eight hours a day in textile mills, and those between 13 and 18 to a maximum of twelve hours. No child was to work at night. Two hours of schooling were to be provided each day, and four factory inspectors were appointed.

The Act was not particularly effective. The manufacturers got round the conditions without much trouble, and four inspectors were nowhere near enough to ensure the conditions of the Act were being followed. But this Act – with its appointment of factory inspectors – marked the start of modern factory legislation.

In 1844, a further Act reduced hours for children under 13 to 6½ per day, either in the morning or afternoon. Children under 18 and women (who were included for the first time) were to work no more than twelve hours a day, with 1½ hours for meals.

In 1847, the campaign for the Ten Hours Movement finally resulted in a Factory Act reducing the hours for women and young people to ten a day, but it wasn't until 1867 that this Act was extended to include non-textile factories and workshops.

In 1901, the minimum working age for all trades was raised to 12, and in 1918 the minimum working age was raised again, after the Fisher Education Act made school compulsory for everyone until the age of 14.

Child labour was a major contributing factor in the growth of the textile industry in Halifax. As we have seen, the employment of little girls in the first half of the nineteenth century was regarded by many mill masters as 'necessary'. James Akroyd died in 1836 and his brother Jonathan took over the business; when Jonathan Akroyd died in 1847, shortly before the Ten Hour Bill was made effective, he left an estate of £1,750,000.

A statue of Oastler with two children, sculpted in bronze by John Birnie Philip, was erected in Bradford in 1869 opposite the then Midland Railway Station. It now stands in Northgate.

Girls at Work in the Mines

The drawing overleaf was made by sub-commissioner Samuel Scriven to illustrate his evidence for the Children's Employment Commission into mine workers in 1842. The drawing was done at Elland, in Ditchforth and Clay's colliery (a Dickensian name, if ever there was one). A woman is hauling two teenagers, Ann Ambler and William Dyson, out of a deep pit shaft. When the teenagers arrive at the top, the woman will make the winch fast and, using brute force alone, will heave them both out, grasping a hand of each.

Samuel Scriven states drily, 'The imperfection of the machinery for descending and ascending the shafts … is stated to be the cause of many accidents… In getting on or off the clatch-iron … you are at the mercy of the winder.'[25]

Scriven recounts how in another mine he'd visited, the winder's attention had been diverted by 'a passing funeral', and how when the teenager reached the top he was drawn right up and over the roller and plunged back into the shaft.

When this drawing appeared in the press in 1842, incredibly to us, outrage wasn't focused on the exhaustion on the faces of the teenagers, or at their perilous situation as they swung about in mid-air. The Victorians' horror was almost entirely due to the fact that a boy and a girl, scantily clad, are sitting crotch to crotch.

Drawing from First Report of the Commissioners (Mines) 1842 p.79

The Children's Employment Commission evolved partly as a result of the fight to secure the minimum ten-hour working day for mill workers, and partly as a result of a terrible accident that had occurred in a pit at Silkstone, Barnsley, on 4 July 1838. Twenty-six children – eleven girls and fifteen boys – drowned during a violent thunderstorm. Many press reports gave a graphic and moving account of how the steam-engine, which should have winched everyone to the top, was unable to function in the rain:

> Forty of the smaller children [which raises the question just how many children were in the mine] were forced to make their way uphill to the 'day-hole' – an opening in a horizontal shaft. There they were met by a deluge of water which swept twenty-six children back into the pit. The children drowned were aged from seven to seventeen.
>
> It was the most heart-rending sight that could be witnessed to see the carts with the bodies in them going through Silkstone, leaving a corpse or two at nearly every door – the women in a state of distraction, tearing the hair from their heads.[26]

This accident brought to public attention the fact that children and infants were working in the pits. Although the coal seams around Halifax were thin and didn't produce much coal, they were near the surface and reasonably accessible. The advent of steam power had brought with it such a great demand for coal it was worth working the seams – especially if labour was cheap.

When 33-year-old Samuel Scriven arrived in Halifax to carry out his investigations, he and his wife stayed at the recently opened Northgate Hotel. (The hotel was demolished in 1959 and is now the site of the Broad Street Plaza.) According to an advertisement in the *Leeds Mercury*, in its heyday the Northgate, with its handsome stone front, had '50 Bed Rooms, several good private Sitting Rooms, good Kitchens, Larders, Cellars, &c' and 'stabling for 60 horses'.[27] It's difficult to imagine Samuel Scriven, as he dined in these luxurious surroundings, discussing with his wife at the end of the day the degradation, danger and appalling inhumanity he had witnessed in the mines just a few miles distant.

Scriven visited at least six local pits, including the Rawsons' mines at Swan Bank, and Stocks' mines at Shaw Lane and Boothtown. He was a conscientious man and went to the lengths of putting on 'a suitable dress of flannel, clogs and kneecaps' in order to descend into the mines himself. In entering into the children's workplace he picked up an extraordinarily vivid picture of their way of life.

One reason for employing children was that the tunnels were small. Scriven reported:

> I know but of two gates that will admit of the use of horses (Messrs. Rawson's Swan Bank and the Junction Pit at Low Moor). In some of them I have had to creep upon my hands and knees the whole distance, the height being barely twenty inches, and then have gone still lower upon my breast, and crawled like a turtle.[28]

Children were employed as 'hurriers' and 'thrusters', pulling and pushing corves (large tubs) of coal for the miners ('getters'). Patience Kershaw, who lived in a terraced house on Ploughcroft Lane and worked at Stocks' mine in Boothtown, gave the following testimony to Scriven:

> My father has been dead about a year; my mother is living and has ten children, five lads and five lasses; the oldest is about thirty, the youngest is four; three lasses go to mill; all the lads are colliers, two getters and three hurriers; one lives at home and does nothing; mother does nought but look after home.

> All my sisters have been hurriers, but three went to the mill. Alice went because her legs swelled from hurrying in cold water when she was hot. I never went to day-school; I go to Sunday-school, but I cannot read or write; I go to pit at five o'clock in the morning and come out at five in the evening; I get my breakfast of porridge and milk first; I take my dinner with me, a cake, and eat it as I go; I do not stop or rest any time for the purpose; I get nothing else until I get home, and then have potatoes and meat, not every day meat. I hurry in the clothes I have now got on, trousers and ragged jacket; the bald place upon my

head is made by thrusting the corves; my legs have never swelled, but sisters' did when they went to mill; I hurry the corves a mile and more underground and back; they weigh 300 cwt.; I hurry 11 a-day; I wear a belt and chain at the workings, to get the corves out; the getters that I work for are naked except their caps; they pull off all their clothes; I see them at work when I go up; sometimes they beat me, if I am not quick enough, with their hands; they strike me upon my back; the boys take liberties with me sometimes they pull me about; I am the only girl in the pit; there are about 20 boys and 15 men; all the men are naked.[29]

When Scriven's report was published in 1842, it was not the fact that Patience worked twelve-hour days, beaten and barely fed, dragging heavy loads to which she was chained like an animal, which caused such moral outrage. It was the fact that she worked beside men who stripped naked.

Thanks to the diligence of Samuel Scriven, we know how some of the girls in Halifax felt about their work in the mines. Here is more of their testimony[30]:

Susan Pitchforth, aged 11, living in Elland:

I run 24 corves a day. I cannot come up until I have done them all. I had rather set cards or anything else than work in the pit.

Selina Ambre, aged 12, Joseph Stocks' pit, Boothtown:

I would rather go to mill than hurry. My uncle could na get a hurrier nowhere, so I had no choice.

Patience Kershaw again:

I would rather work in mill than in coal-pit.

Margaret Gormley, aged 9, 'or going on nine', who worked in Lindley, Huddersfield, stated:

> I have been at work in the pit thrusting corves about a
> year ... I had rather lake [play] than go into the pit. I had
> rather set cards than go into the pit.

These were the views of the girls. The views of their mothers were not asked. Some – such as Patience Kershaw's mother – were widows and desperately needed the money. Others may have felt obliged by male members of the family to send the girls to work for them.

Regarding the views of the wealthier women of Halifax, we're fortunate to have the voice of at least one upper-middle-class Halifax woman that still speaks to us clearly across the years. Anne Lister, of Shibden Hall, herself owned several small collieries, including Listerwick. (Note: Anne died in Russia in 1840, before Scriven's visit to Halifax.)

Anne Lister was motivated in just the same way as the male mine owners around her – by a desire to maximise profits. She appears to have used the fact that she was a woman – and therefore underestimated by her male peers – to ask guileless questions and so dupe local mine owners into giving her valuable commercial information. She spent some time questioning Joseph Stocks, for example (the same Stocks who employed Patience Kershaw). He told Lister exactly how much coal he produced and what he sold it for.

Lister wrote, 'I then turned to my calculations. If the coal costs $3\frac{1}{2}d$ a corve getting and hurrying, the clear gain would be £453.15s per acre ...'[31]

This calculation included the miners' and children's wages. Lister, just like the male mine owners in Halifax, was making a tidy profit from their labour – a profit which she intended to use to maintain her social standing.

Lister went on another fact-finding mission to Binns Bottom mine at Southowram. Here, she showed no fear about descending into a filthy, dangerous mine-working, nor was she shocked to come across naked men. She merely says matter-of-factly that she could:

walk upright in the shaft 300 yards long … [I was] about ½ hour in the works. 4 men getting coal – 1 man will get about 20 corves in 5 hours… Gave the banksman 2/- for himself & 2/- for the 4 men who worked naked.[32]

Lister makes no mention of seeing children at work, but that may simply have been that the children didn't interest her. The only thing that did interest her – and the only thing that interested her male peers – was how much coal could be brought out, and at what price. As a businesswoman, Lister was remarkably shrewd. She also recognised no difference between herself and a man when conducting business. She recounts how Jeremiah Rawson told her, 'he was never beaten but by ladies, & I had beaten him. Said I gravely, "It is the intellectual part of us that makes a bargain, and that has no sex, or ought to have none."'[33]

Anne Lister's diaries show her to be quick-witted and intelligent, but they also show her to be remarkably self-absorbed. In this callous entry regarding a mining accident, she says: '2 men killed in Mr Rawson's pit at the top of the hill… Yesterday ½ hour asleep on the sofa.'[34]

There is no record of how the other middle-class women in Lister's circle reacted to the death of two colliers. Quite possibly they would have found it equally unworthy of note. However, the accident at Silkstone colliery three years later in which twenty-six children died did send shockwaves through the nation, moving even Queen Victoria to take notice.

The number of girls employed in mines in Halifax – and across Yorkshire – was small in comparison to the vast numbers employed in the textile industry, but the testimony of the likes of Patience Kershaw of Ploughcroft Lane led to the Mines and Collieries Regulation Act of 1842, banning the employment of all women and girls underground and of boys under 10. This Act was a revolutionary piece of legislation. With the rise of industrialisation, legislators had been pressurised by public opinion to become socially responsible.

After the legislation was passed, what of the mining girls and women who were now out of work? They were not offered any financial compensation for the loss of their jobs. The eleven men who investigated their plight, and the men who drafted the subsequent legislation, failed to consider the impact of the new laws on the lives of these women and girls, or to consider the necessity that had driven them to this dangerous occupation in the first place. Many women across the country continued to work in the mines because they needed the money – only now they suffered the added danger of being discovered and forced to pay the mine owner's fine for breaking the law.

Patience Kershaw of Ploughcroft Lane left the mines to become a wool-comber at Illingworth before taking work as a servant and then a washerwoman. In 1867, she entered the workhouse in Halifax. In December that year she was admitted to the West Riding Pauper Lunatic Asylum in Wakefield, where her notes give the pitiful record that she believed, 'Jack and his dogs are always in her bedroom at night and won't allow her to sleep'. Patience, whose testimony had contributed to a revolutionary change in employment law, died in the asylum on 12 March 1869.[35]

CHAPTER TWO

An Unequal Education

The Early Years

In 1800, a 10-year-old girl setting cards in Halifax might very well not be able to spell her name. Girls from middle-class families fared better in terms of education, but they rarely reached the same level as their brothers.

In 1950, all girls of 10 in Halifax were in full-time education, schooling until 15 was compulsory and free, and universities were open to women. The educational opportunities that expanded for women during these 150 years arguably revolutionised their lives more than anything else in this period.

Sunday Schools

'Hundreds of men eminent in literature, science and art, owe their position to the godly training received in our Sabbath Schools.'

So said Reverend John Naylor of the Halifax Sunday School Union in 1913.[1] Sunday Schools may have benefited the eminent men of Halifax, but they almost certainly made more difference to the women. At a time when education had to be paid for, if a family had to choose between schooling a son or a daughter, they would choose the son. Girls were needed to help in the home, or else their wages were necessary to the household. Sunday Schools provided a free place, outside their working week, where girls could learn to read.

Battledore. Rare Books PE1118 .E58 tiny. Division of Rare and Manuscript Collections, Cornell University

By the middle of the nineteenth century, the Halifax Sunday School Union was made up of fifty schools. Forty-seven of the schools had libraries, and their total number of books – in many cases free to borrow – was an astonishing 17,000. A remarkable number of children were prepared to walk a long way to learn to read. In 1830, 600 pupils attended Mount Zion Sunday School.[2]

The importance of the Sunday School movement can be seen in the immense popularity of the Sunday School Jubilees, which were held in the Piece Hall. In 1890, tens of thousands of visitors arrived by train and vast crowds formed outside. A great trade was done in telescopes, so that those without tickets could watch from the house tops or from the slopes of Beacon Hill. Almost 30,000 Sunday School scholars crowded the Piece Hall. They were given a currant bun each and over 80,000 of these buns were consumed on the day.[3]

Although Sunday Schools were often organised and taught by female volunteers, sadly there is little record left of these women's voices. When we do catch a glimpse of them, they provide a refreshing and illuminating picture of their community. In a performance at Roomfield Baptist Church in Todmorden in 1908, the women sang a comic song about the men's contribution (or lack of it):

> In Sunday School they're again behind,
> For not one in ten has a strong enough mind,
> To teach a class of boys of age from six to ten,
> So the ladies have to come to the rescue again.[4]

This was at the turn of the twentieth century, just as women's voices began to be heard more often, but also at this time the

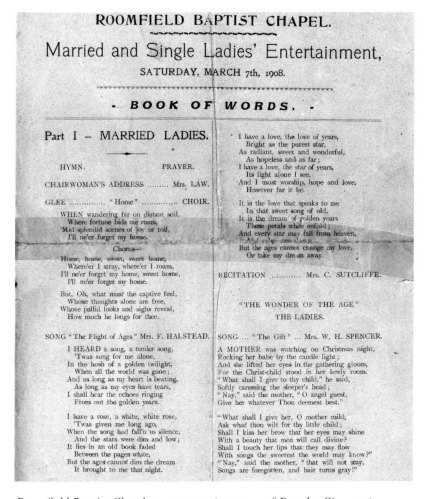

Roomfield Baptist Church programme (courtesy of Douglas Simpson)

popularity of Sunday Schools was in decline. There were a number of reasons for this. The restriction on children's working hours allowed them to attend school classes in the week, which by the turn of the twentieth century were free at elementary level. At Mount Zion in 1915, just 123 scholars were recorded in the Sunday School, compared to the 600 they'd had in 1830.

In 1913, the Reverend Naylor spoke of the Sunday School movement as, 'one of the greatest forces moulding our national character', adding that, 'men and women of the best type had

Women Outside Mount Zion Chapel, Mytholmroyd PHDA/Hebden Bridge Local History Soc HLS01514

come forward to give their time and talent'.[5] Without a doubt, the girls of Halifax in the nineteenth century benefited from the vast service rendered to their education by the non-conformist movement and its Sunday Schools.

Dame Schools, Charity Schools and Mill Schools

At the start of the nineteenth century, elementary education in Halifax, as in many other towns, was a haphazard jumble of various establishments – some better than others. Dame schools, which were usually run by women in their own homes, charged a small fee. In working-class communities they were mainly attended by infants still too young to earn a wage. The quality of education provided varied greatly, and often they were simply a convenient form of childcare for mothers who needed to work.

Dame schools for middle-class children were more exclusive, but not necessarily better. Anne Lister was sent away to a dame school in Ripon. She later explained she was, 'sent to school early because they could do nothing with me at home, and whipped every day, except now & then in the holidays, for two years.'[6]

Lister described herself at that age as 'a curious genius' and full of high spirits. The whippings she endured at school were perhaps an attempt to make her conform and be more docile, as required of a girl. Anyone who has read Lister's diaries will know this attempt failed.[7]

Once working-class girls began to work, they had no access to education apart from the Sunday Schools. After the 1833 Factory Act, employers were obliged to ensure that the children working in their mills had two hours' schooling per day (extended to three hours with the 1844 Act). Edward Akroyd ran schools in his mills at Haley Hill and Copley. Here, over a thousand 'half-timers' paid two pence a week out of their wages for their education. It's debatable how much these children could learn after an exhausting shift, but girls in Halifax schools fared much better than others in Yorkshire. The Schools' Inquiry Commission in 1868 found that of the four towns investigated in Yorkshire (York, Selby, Sheffield and Halifax),

> by far the highest rate of school attendance is attained in Halifax, where the Factory Act is efficacious not only in enforcing the attendance of the half-timers, but also in giving to the whole industrial population more orderly and punctual habits, and a stronger sense of the importance of education.[8]

The 'orderly and punctual habits' of the Halifax population didn't just arise from the Factory Act. As with the Sunday Schools, women played a significant role behind the scenes in many charity schools in Halifax. A British School, run by the nonconformist British and Foreign School Society, opened in Halifax in 1813,

Esther Blakey, Wings Newsletter Oct 1900 (Calderdale Libraries)

moving to Great Albion Street in 1820. Esther Blakey sat on the girls' committee for the school and was one of its most active members. She lived with her husband, a mill owner, and their three children, along with their two servants, in a large house in Trinity Place. Esther was a Quaker, and this religious organisation was known for its progressive views on women's education. Like many middle-class women of her time, Esther Blakey did much work for charity. Her particular causes were the Temperance movement, the Anti-Slavery Movement, and the Peace and the Anti-Opium Societies.[9]

In his report to the Schools Inquiry Commissioners of 1868, Joshua Fitch found that on the whole elementary education for girls from poorer families in Halifax was of 'an efficient kind', and that at this level the girls' education was the same as the boys', 'with the exception of sewing'.[10]

Early years' education was still haphazard, however. The Forster Education Act of 1870 was the first of a number of acts to attempt to regularise elementary education and to ensure all children aged 5 to 13 had free access to it. For the first time, women were able to play a civic role in education. They had the right both to vote for and to serve on the new School Boards. At Halifax's first contested School Board election, in January 1874, no women were nominated, but the election caused great excitement in the town; 10,000 votes were recorded at the twenty-four ballot booths provided.[11] With this rare opportunity to cast their vote, women must have been a significant factor in the vast turnout. However, the first woman wasn't elected to the Halifax School Board until 1892, when Mrs Nathan Whitley took the place of her late husband.

The new Halifax School Board laid down salaries for teachers as follows: masters £120 per annum, mistresses £80 per annum; assistant masters £52 per annum, assistant mistresses £35 per annum. Even the apprentice boy teachers earned more than their female counterparts, with a 13-year-old male pupil teacher earning £15, and a 13-year-old female earning £12.10.[12]

After the Balfour Education Act of 1902, School Boards were replaced by Education Committees. Each committee was obliged to have at least one woman member. It was a start, but despite their female member, in Halifax in 1904 ten annual scholarships were offered to boys of low-income families to attend Heath Grammar School.[13] There were no scholarships offered to girls – this despite the fact that Heath Grammar was in contravention of its statute by only accepting boys, as shall be seen in the section on secondary education.

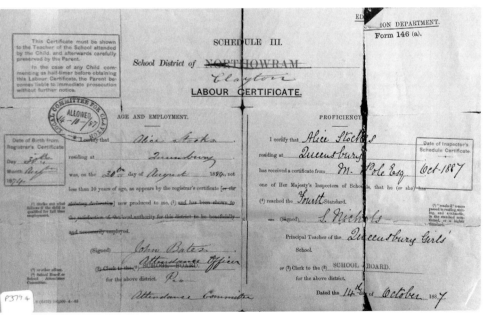

13-year-old Alice Stocks' half-timer certificate showing proof of age (Calderdale Libraries)

At the start of the twentieth century, girls working half-time in the mills continued to fall behind in school compared to full-timers. Many teachers did their best to help. Miss Leeming, who was head of St Augustine's Girls' School in 1915, found the half-timers so sleepy she started gardening classes for the girls to let them get some fresh air.[14] 'Half-time' education continued until the school-leaving age was raised from 12 to 14, when the 1918 Fisher Education Act was fully implemented in 1921. It seems inconceivable to us today that young children were still working in factories well into the twentieth century, but this practice was accepted in its day. Often the girls felt a sense of pride in their ability to earn. One girl at St Augustine's described, 'how she pressed her parents to be allowed to go to the mill, so that she might contribute to the family budget … and how proudly she set out for home clasping her first week's wage of 1/6.'[15]

The 1921 Education Act meant parents had a duty to ensure their children received an education until the age of 14, but girls often continued to be kept at home to help with chores or with younger siblings, while their brothers were sent to school.

The 1944 Education Act paved the way for the eleven-plus and raised the school-leaving age to 15.

Although Joshua Fitch had called elementary education for girls in Halifax 'efficient', their secondary education was a different matter. The findings of Fitch and his fellow commissioners were shocking and caused a national debate.

'A cruel injustice.' The Schools Inquiry Commission 1867-68 and the findings on girls' secondary education in Halifax

As we've seen, in the nineteenth century, even more so than today, education in Britain was divided entirely along class and gender lines. Even liberal campaigners for girls' education such as Dorothy Beale accepted that working-class girls would leave school after elementary education. Secondary schools were the preserve of girls from middle-class families. Girls from wealthy and aristocratic families were generally educated at home.

In the early nineteenth century the daughters of Jeremiah Rawson were educated by a governess, Miss King, at their home at Shay House in Halifax. Miss King was said to be 'a very charming lady'.[16] We know nothing else about Miss King's qualifications or what she taught her girls, but it's likely that the Rawsons required little more from their daughters than that they, too, should learn to be charming.

In the 1860s, there were thirteen private day and boarding schools for middle-class girls in Halifax.[17] These girls' schools were much smaller than those for boys. This was partly because parents wanted something more 'home-like' for their daughters, and partly because a small school gave the impression of exclusivity. Schools Commissioner Fitch was not impressed. In his opinion, the schools' small size contributed to the narrowness of the girls' education. He reported that in the West Riding, 'all the sharp lines of demarcation which divide society into classes, and all the jealousies and suspicions which help keep these classes apart, are seen in their fullest operation in girls' schools.'[18]

Girls' schools tended to offer a basic curriculum of reading and needlework, along with 'elegant accomplishments' such as French, drawing, music and dancing. In 1851, Jane Walton ran a ladies' boarding school at St John's House on Trinity Road. Miss Walton's School had thirty-two pupils at the time, the majority of whom were from the Halifax area, but many came from the south of England, and one from as far as Montreal.[19] We know nothing now of the quality of the lessons in Miss Walton's school, but it's likely the

Miss King (H. Ling Roth Yorkshire Coiners)

standard was not high, particularly for the older pupils. Even where teachers wanted to encourage the older girls, they were often thwarted by the parents, whose main concern was for their daughters to become accomplished enough to attract a husband.

Unitarian schools were among the few establishments to offer girls something intellectually stimulating. Here non-conformism again proves a positive influence. Martha and Hannah Mellin were sisters belonging to Northgate End Chapel. In the late eighteenth century they ran a girls' academy with an emphasis on intellectual development. Dorothy Wordsworth was a pupil and Anne Lister later attended some lessons as a day pupil. In 1814, the Mellins' academy was acquired by Hannah and Elizabeth Watkinson, where it was run at New Road, Ward's End, before moving to Carlton Street. Anne Lister records seeing the girls from the Misses Watkinsons' school lining the front bench at a lecture on chemistry and natural philosophy at the Assembly Room in Talbot Yard.

But schools like the Watkinsons' were the exception. Joshua Fitch found that at elementary level girls in the West Riding held their own, and often surpassed the boys, but by the time they were 12 they were told, 'that Latin is not a feminine acquirement; that arithmetic and mathematics are only fit for boys; that science is not useful to a woman; and that she must begin to devote her attention to "ladylike accomplishments".'[20]

Most of this was down to the parents' expectations. Almost all of the teachers Fitch spoke to reported their dismay. One teacher said baldly, 'I believe that girls in England have not had a fair chance.'[21]

Endowed schools – that is, schools such as Heath Grammar, which had been established through a charitable endowment from a benefactor – were particularly singled out by the Commission for failing girls. Fitch wrote, 'It is impossible to make a survey of the state of the ancient educational endowments of this district without being struck by the fact of the total exclusion of girls from all their advantages.'[22]

When a benefactor left an endowment for a school, there would be a legal statute drawn up detailing his or her intentions. In some cases girls were specifically excluded. When Grace Ramsden left an endowment for her school in Elland, she stated it was for 'poor boys of the Township'.[23] She left no provision for girls. However, in almost every case girls were not excluded – and yet over the years most of these endowed schools began to take in boys only. Brooksbank School in Elland, for example, was established by a charitable endowment in 1712 to teach both boys and girls, but by 1829 only boys attended.[24]

The schools inquiry noted there were two endowed secondary schools in Halifax Parish – Hipperholme Grammar School and Heath Grammar School. Neither of these secondary schools took in girls, yet Heath Grammar School's statute clearly stated that the school was for, 'The admission and teaching of every scholar of the town and parish of Halifax, of what condition soever, nothing shall be demanded.'[25] The statute can still be seen in Crossley Heath School's archives today.

The only endowed secondary school in the West Riding to take in girls was at Rishworth. Even here, Fitch reported with dismay that their education was not equal to that of the boys:

> The boys are retained until 16 years of age and receive an education to prepare them for the University. The girls, however, are required to quit school at 14. A plain, domestic education is provided for them... It does not offer even to one of these girls ... the opportunity of qualifying herself as a governess or proceeding to a place of higher education ... it is nevertheless the only endowed school in the district that attempts to do anything for them whatever.[26]

The commissioners across Yorkshire made their feelings clear in the strongest terms. This exclusion of girls from endowed schools was, 'in the highest degree inexpedient and unjust... Appropriation of almost all the Educational Endowments of the

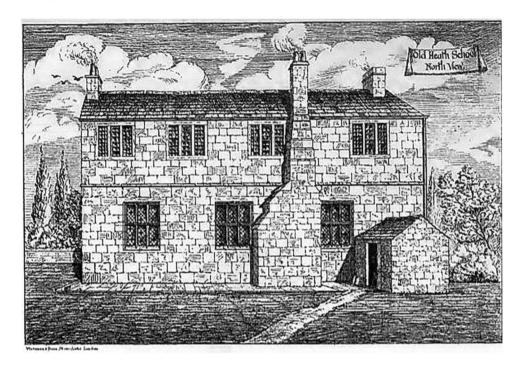

Heath School in 1870 (Thomas Cox The Grammar School of Queen Elizabeth at Heath nr Halifax *1879)*

county to the education of boys is felt by a large and increasing number, both of men and women, to be a cruel injustice.'[27]

After the findings of the Schools Inquiry were published, the abysmal provision of education for girls in England became an urgent topic of conversation nationwide. The inquiry was swiftly followed by the 1869 Endowed Schools Act, one of whose aims was to extend the benefits of endowments to girls 'as far as conveniently may be'. Not much changed, however, and schools such as Heath Grammar School continued to take in boys only.

On 21 October 1870, a meeting took place in York to discuss the 1869 Act and 'Middle-Class Education in Yorkshire'. The Archbishop of York talked at length about the need for educational reform. Buried in his speech is a very brief mention of the girls:

Education for one sex to the exclusion of education of the other was a preposterous idea which had only been tolerated because people had become accustomed to it; if anybody would show the way to remedy so ridiculous and absurd an injustice they would welcome the information.[28]

Reading this account from a modern perspective, one can't help being struck by the fact that the Archbishop is asking for advice on remedying inequality, yet he invited fourteen men to sit with him on the platform, and not one woman. The newspaper report calls the audience 'decidedly representative', but it goes on to list only the influential men present, adding as an afterthought that there were also 'several ladies'. A government inquiry had revealed in the strongest terms that girls' education was unequal and unjust, and yet no women teaching professionals were given a voice in this subsequent discussion.

It is no wonder, then, that women in Yorkshire went on to take matters into their own hands. The Yorkshire Ladies Council of Education was set up in 1871. Its aims were to promote, 'the higher education of girls, and to assist girls in preparing for examinations in the higher branches of knowledge.'[29]

This project by the Yorkshire ladies led to the founding of Halifax High School for Girls.

Halifax High School for Girls

In 1876, Mrs Nathan Whitley (who would later sit on the Halifax School Board) reported to the Yorkshire Ladies Council of Education that, 'It is intended during the present year to agitate the town [of Halifax] for a middle-class girls' school, to be established by means of a company.'[30]

Halifax Girls' High School was opened in January 1877 at Savile Hall. In 1878, Mrs Edward Crossley reported that the school 'was now on a working basis and took in around 150 pupils'.[31]

The new girls' school thrived. Phyllis Bentley described it at as being, at the end of the nineteenth century, 'a newish, pioneer

Phyllis Bentley in 1957 (Calderdale Libraries)

establishment... The headmistress, Miss Ellen Bolton, was an educational pioneer; a tall, fine, eager, intelligent, warm-hearted woman, an excellent organiser immensely keen to give Halifax girls the opportunity for a decent education.'

The opening of the school in Halifax was an important step, but there was still a very long way to go until girls' education was taken as seriously as the boys'. Unlike her brothers, but like many other girls, Bentley was expected to miss school whenever there were:

> domestic upsets, a maid leaving unexpectedly or the like ... I suffered severely; it was my duty no doubt to stay at home and help to wash up and dust and lay tables, and of course I must do my duty, but I felt that I was behind

bars, irretrievably cut off from everything which made life worth living.[32]

Having to miss school was almost a painful experience for Bentley and caused her a lifelong hatred of housework. She later came to equate marriage with domesticity and a lack of intellectual fulfilment; she remained single all her life.

Bentley recalls her academic successes with pride, but in a way that no boy of the time would ever have had to consider. 'The taking of examinations by girls was a blow struck for the emancipation of women, and a right which had to be fought for; it was our joy and duty to show that we were as clever as any boy.'[33]

The High School continued to thrive, and in the 1920s the school had outgrown its premises. In June 1930, Mrs Howard Clay laid the foundation stone for a new school at Craven

Form Room at Princess Mary's (School Brochure 1931. Calderdale Libraries)

Lodge. This school would merge the Girls' High School with the Girls' Secondary School. (The Girls' Secondary School had also grown and operated from two buildings – one on Prescott Street and one at Craven Lodge. The latter was demolished to make way for the new premises.) The new school was opened in 1931 by Princess Mary and became Princess Mary's School.

Although sad at the demolition of their 'fine old building' at Craven Lodge, the Secondary School's headmistress, D. M. Scott, who became head of Princess Mary's, called the new building, with its science labs, gymnasium, music and domestic science rooms, 'one of the finest schools in England'. [34]

I must mention here what a delight it is, and how moving, to come across the voices of the girls themselves in the records left by Halifax Girls' High and Secondary Schools during this period. It is as though the girls finally have a say in the archives, after centuries of silence. Finding their bright, humorous voices – still as lively as ever after almost a century – makes the terrible injustice dealt all those girls previously lacking an education all the more heart-breaking.

Girls and Staff of Princess Mary's, 1934 (Calderdale Libraries)

Here is part of a story from the 1931 Halifax Girls' Secondary School magazine, entitled 'Washing Up':

> '—*the old castle was steeped in darkness. A shot rang—* *then silence. A black shadow flitted—*' Oh! There's mother calling. I wonder what she wants me for. I hope she wants me to wash up … I much prefer washing up to reading, and I'm certain that every other girl does.

Unfortunately, girls were all too often required to drop their studies and help with the washing up.

The Focus on Domestic Science

At a school speech in 1939, educationalist Miss Cumberbatch advised the girls leaving Princess Mary's to practise, 'the virtues of strength and gentleness … cheerfulness, good humour, gratitude, courtesy and consideration.'[35] A century earlier, Samuel Dunn, a Wesleyan Minister who preached in Halifax, wrote a pamphlet called, *A Present for Female Servants, or The Secret of their Getting and Keeping Good Places*. His list of the virtues necessary in a good servant is strikingly similar. It included, 'obedience, respectfulness, kindness, diligence, honesty, truthfulness, modesty, patience and thankfulness.'[36]

Although educational opportunities for girls had expanded, girls were still expected to leave school for a life of domestic service – that is, a life running the household for their husbands and families.

Crossley Orphanage was founded by the three Crossley brothers in 1864. The boys at the orphanage school were able to take Latin and advanced arithmetic, plus a modern language, while the girls concentrated on needlework and 'useful departments of household service'.[37] After the findings of the 1860s Schools Inquiry, education for girls at the orphanage improved. In 1880, when Miss Angela Collins was headmistress, she placed science at the forefront of the girls' curriculum. Under her headship, there were few failures in the Cambridge Local

Advertisement for School Coats (Halifax Secondary School for Girls Brochure 1931. Calderdale Libraries)

examinations, and some of the girls at the school reportedly scored the highest marks in the country.[38]

Unfortunately, although she was a pioneering teacher, Miss Collins, too, was tied by the social conventions of the time. She had to resign in 1892 because she was about to get married.

Crossley Orphanage went on to become the Crossley and Porter Orphan Home and School. There were effectively two schools in one building, with the girls' school facing Skircoat Moor Road. The girls' headmistress, Miss Richardson, reported at the July 1939 speech day that nursing and domestic science were still the girls' 'favourite careers' on leaving.[39] This is hardly surprising, since this is what they'd mainly been educated for.

Rita Humphreys was a boarder at Blue Coats School in Halifax during the 1930s. In June 1934, the rules of the school

DOMESTIC SCIENCE

Domestic Science Room at Princess Mary's (School Brochure 1931. Calderdale Libraries)

stated: 'From 14 to 16 the girls are trained in domestic service in all branches of household work. The Ladies' Committee will gladly help any who wish to obtain good situations.'

After 14, scholarships were available from the Blue Coat charity to send pupils on to Heath Grammar School, but of course these scholarships were only available to the boys. From 14 the girls at Blue Coats had to help out in the running of the orphanage, including the laundry, which in those days was a monumental task:

> A huge copper stood in one corner of the washing cellar… There was a hand operated washing machine with a paddle affair inside which rotated back and forth knocking the stuffing out of the woollen vests. We stood at long shallow stone sinks with huge pieces of hard yellow soap and scrubbing brushes. We scrubbed away at knickers, underpants, chemises and shirts… The mangle was a formidable machine with huge wooden rollers. We had to turn the handle while Mrs G fed the beast with clothing.[40]

When the Blue Coats School's chaplain declared he needed 'a girl' for his household in Ilkley, Rita Humphreys was put forward for the position. She accepted with a complete lack of enthusiasm, but this was the type of role she'd been trained for, and she had little other option.

Ovenden Senior School (later the Secondary School, then the High School, and then the Ridings) opened in 1937. The school had what was then state-of-the-art equipment, with a gym, swimming baths, woodwork and metalwork rooms for the boys, and a domestic science class and a complete 'housewifery flat' for the girls. The housewifery flat contained a living-room and dining area, a bedroom, kitchen and bathroom, and was furnished like a small home. Four girls at a time would spend the whole day managing the house, including cleaning it, learning about buying food and provision of meals, etc.

Girls sewing at Ovenden Senior School (School Brochure 1937. Calderdale Libraries)

These 'housewifery' skills were undoubtedly useful, but when the focus of their education was on the domestic rather than a broad range of subjects, girls missed out. Because lessons were divided on gender lines, the boys missed out, too. One former pupil at Ovenden in the 1960s recalled, 'Unusually for the time we had a boy who wanted to learn cooking. We were so cruel to him; sorry, Derek.'[41]

Secondary education for girls in Halifax improved dramatically after the Schools Inquiry Commission of the 1860s, but girls' education continued to focus on the domestic rather than the academic for decades to follow. Since women in 1950 were often obliged to give up work when they married, their education was still considered by many not to be as important as their brothers'.

Further Education: the Halifax girls 'not burdened with a serious education'

If secondary education for girls in Halifax was poor in the nineteenth century, further education was almost non-existent.

Anne Lister was unusual in that she sought out lessons from her local vicar, the Reverend Knight, and that she had the means to pay him. Lister was energetic and ambitious, and her determination to improve her mind is admirable. She writes, 'Went to Mr Knight's & sat ½ hour. Mentioning my despair of getting on with my studies, he proposed my giving up altogether the thought of pursuing them. This, I did not think it necessary to dissemble, I scouted entirely.'[42]

To 'scout' meant to treat with scorn. It took a woman of Lister's strength of character to persist in her studies. Without support, and actively discouraged from learning, it's hardly surprising that many women conformed to society's low expectations of them. Lister's friend, Miss Browne, bemoans the fact that she can't read as many books as she'd like. Her mother, 'did not like to see her poring over books in the daytime, but that she was kept stitching and attending to domestic concerns', and that she is 'forced to read by stealth'.[43]

The Northgate End chapel again stood out by establishing a Book Society for both men and women, but since the subscription cost eight shillings per year, membership was restricted to those few who could afford it. The Society met once a month at one of the houses to discuss that month's books and periodicals.[44] This must have been an important event in the women's social calendar, as it provided one of their few opportunities to debate the news and cultural affairs of the day as equals with the men.

Anne Lister mentions this Book Society and how she was invited to join it by Edward Priestley. She declined, telling Priestley she went often to the Halifax library '& had there as much reading as I had time for'.[45] It's hard to imagine forthright Anne Lister doing the rounds of hosting the Book Society and making sure enough tea and cake was served. However, Lister did become one of the twelve subscribers who paid £100 each for the Literary and Philosophical Society's Museum building on Harrison Road. Here again she stands out: 'I laughed on looking over the list [of subscribers] and finding myself the only lady.'[46]

Ventures such as the Book Society were for the middle classes. Halifax Young Women's Institute and Halifax Working Men's College were founded by Edward Akroyd 'to supplement the education given to the young in the factories and national schools'.[47]

The women's classes were not intended for academic study, but for promoting, 'the cultivation of domestic arts which were too often neglected in the manufacturing districts'.[48]

In April 1861, there was a prize day at the institute at Haley Hill. The young men were awarded prizes for, 'Scripture, arithmetic, English literature and grammar, geography, history, French, chemistry and physics'. The young women, on the other hand, were given prizes for 'needlework, knitting, regularity of attendance, &c'.[49]

In other words, the women were dismissed with an 'etc.' and that notorious consolation prize – a prize for turning up. Ironically, by underestimating the women's intellectual capabilities, Akroyd also overlooked a potential resource for improving his own business. At the 1872 prize-giving he expressed his disappointment that so few of the male students were interested in science, telling them, 'there was hardly a branch of industry carried on [in Halifax] in which material benefit would not accrue from the study of chemistry.'[50]

Chemists and engineers were vital to innovation in the textile industry and to staying ahead of the competition. If not enough young men in Halifax were interested, it does seem a dreadful waste not to have educated the women in the subjects.

One interesting fact to emerge from the Schools Inquiry of the 1860s is that some of the girls from Halifax were highly talented artists. In this subject at least their skills were recognised and developed.

Charles Fox, of the School of Art at the Mechanics' Institute, told the Commission:

'The young ladies are extremely anxious to learn ... and as a rule are not at all wishful to make mere show drawings, but really apply themselves to learn the principles of art thoroughly.'

One of the girls sold her work at exhibitions, and several others exhibited around the county, winning, 'a very large share of the department's medals and prizes'.[51]

Mr Fox seems almost surprised that the young women were so 'extremely anxious to learn', but their thirst for knowledge was just a tiny proportion of the thirst of the thousands of girls of the time who must have longed to be educated in many other subjects.

Girton College opened its doors to women students in 1869, but girls would continue to face obstacles on the way to further education for many, many years. In the early twentieth century, Janet Cockcroft, who was brought up in Scotland before moving to Halifax, told her headmaster she wanted to study medicine. His reply was, 'Don't be ridiculous. Girls don't go in for sciences.'[52]

Dr Janet Cockcroft on graduating (Photo Philip Cockcroft and Pennine Horizons Digital Archive)

Cockcroft held her ground, but as the only girl at her school to study sciences she endured 'some dreadful teasing'. The quota for women students at Glasgow University in the 1920s was just ten per cent, which meant Cockcroft had to fight harder than the boys to gain a place. Once at university, Janet Cockcroft's struggle continued, and as one of the few female students she was often singled out by the tutors for criticism. It takes someone of enormous strength of character to carry on in these circumstances. Dr Cockcroft rose to the challenge: 'At first it made me furious to be laughed at, so I just worked harder not to make the same mistakes again.'[53]

Faced with challenges such as these on the route to higher education, it's hardly surprising that Phyllis Bentley later wrote, 'It will convey a striking notion of the difference in provincial women's education between 1914 and 1960 … if I mention that I was the first girl among our acquaintance in Halifax to take a University degree.'[54]

After completing her brilliant academic career, Phyllis Bentley was still expected simply to come home and help her mother run the household: 'I attended classes at the Technical College [Calderdale College] on Home Management, and strove earnestly to be "useful in the home".'[55]

Betty Hoyle was a mill owner's daughter from Halifax. In 1939 she married Paul Bryan, who later stood as MP for Sowerby. Paul Bryan once claimed, 'the daughters of the Halifax manufacturing elite "were not burdened with a serious education".'[56]

Paul Bryan graduated from Cambridge in the 1930s. At this time, the institution would still not allow his fellow female students to graduate with a full degree.

Lucy Hutchinson was born on Corporation Street in Halifax in 1870. Hutchinson's father was a manufacturer of cigars, employing around thirty staff. His income wouldn't have been enough to send all five of his children away to school, but luckily for Hutchinson she was born at a time when she could attend the new Halifax Girls' High School. On finishing school, Hutchinson was one of the first two Halifax women to be admitted to Cambridge. Although she passed her finals, as a woman she was not entitled to graduate with a full degree. Educated for a life of domesticity, unlike Paul Bryan, Lucy Hutchinson did not go on to have a distinguished career, despite the 'unusual brilliance' her friends recalled her showing at school.[57] It wasn't until 1948, when Hutchinson was 78, that Cambridge changed the rules and awarded her a full degree. Bryan, who was more than forty years her junior, had been allowed to graduate almost twenty years before her.

These sorts of circumstances and challenges were responsible for the fact that many girls in Halifax in this period – and across the whole country – were not 'burdened by a serious education', despite their willingness to learn.

CHAPTER THREE

Women's Health and Domestic Lives

Women's Chores in the Home

At the beginning of the nineteenth century, the amount of cleaning working-class women were faced with must have been well-nigh insurmountable. Most of the streets in Halifax were unpaved and filthy. When new houses were built, there would be a recess made beside every doorstep to contain an iron boot-scraper:

> Everyone had to scrape the thick mud off his boots before he entered, because the streets were very filthy, as they were un-paved and seldom swept. Even so late as 1872, the newspapers recording the funeral of Sir Francis Crossley mention the fact that many of the elderly gentlemen could not walk in the procession, because of the dirty condition of the roads.[1]

Water shortages compounded the problem as the town expanded rapidly. In the 1840s,

> Water was so scarce one alderman said that people told him they had to steal it. About eight hundred people depended on a dropping-well near Berry Lane... Many people had to go half-a-mile for water, and some declared they were not able to get their breakfast until after mid-day for want of water. Others were up at two

o'clock in the morning to be first at the well, and women often wasted three and four hours a day fetching water.[2]

The lack of toilets (privies) and an adequate sewerage system were a major problem.

On 10 January 1851, a petition was presented to the Board of Health regarding the condition of the town. More than a tenth of the ratepayers signed, but non-ratepayers and all women were barred from adding their signatures. Since women – especially poorer women – were responsible for fetching water, for keeping their houses clean and their children healthy, if they'd been permitted to sign, the number of signatures would have been significantly higher.

Following the petition, engineer William Ranger was sent to Halifax to report on sanitary conditions. His findings were grim:

> With respect to the houses of the poor in Halifax, they are frequently closely built, badly ventilated, and abounding in accumulations of offensive matter… Many families are obliged to occupy but one room for both living and sleeping in, and the consequence is that the inmates are breathing a vitiated and unhealthy atmosphere… It is difficult to suggest a remedy [because] it is generally the result of poverty and not of inclination on the part of the inhabitants.[3]

It is interesting that Ranger says these squalid living conditions were not the fault of the inhabitants. Other commentators have noted how the working class of Halifax and surrounding area – and the women in particular – worked industriously to keep their homes clean. Commissioner James Smith, in his 1845 *Report on the Condition of the Town of Halifax*, stated: 'I found that the people of Halifax use water more liberally for washing their windows and floors … than in any other town I visited.'[4]

By 'people' the commissioner almost certainly meant 'women'. It was highly unlikely the men in the households would have taken responsibility for washing the floors. More than fifty years later, in 1904, Ada Nield Chew – a women's trade-union organiser from Lancashire – also spoke of the industriousness of the women of the Calder Valley, saying it was almost impossible 'to get a meeting anywhere in these parts on a Friday night (cleaning night)'.[5]

As the nineteenth century progressed, living conditions gradually improved, but even with better sanitation and water supply, cleaning remained a constant drudgery. Even up until the 1950s, just washing the household's clothes could take an entire day.

Dyso saves your Labour.

IT isn't always the hardest scrubbing that makes the cleanest floors! Put a spoonful or two of Dyso in the cleaning water, and see how easily Woodwork and Linoleums can be made spotless. Dyso is a real Home labour-saver. Rich in Ammonia, the active cleanser, it simply drives dirt away . . . and always in the shortest time possible.

Buy a two-penny packet of Dyso to-day. It will reduce your Housework by half.

FREE.—Large tins of Delicious Toffee. Children! Collect the Picture Cards from DYSO Packets. Send them to the mothers, in exchange for a large tin of Delicious Toffee. Full particulars on each card.

Dyson's Ammonia Wash Powder

Proprietors: *Thos. Hedley & Co., Ltd., Newcastle-on-Tyne* (also makers of the popular " Fairy " Soap).

Yorkshire Evening Post advertisement Dec 22nd 1926

One Calderdale woman recalled:

> I well remember washday with the tub, mangle and
> the three legged dolly. We would be out of bed at 5 am
> and set the water to boil on the black leaded fire range.
> When it was boiling, we used ladling cans to get it into
> the tub. All whites had to be boiled… If the weather was
> wet, clothes had to be dried inside on the creel or on
> the window ledge and the whole house would be full of
> steam. The day after, the ironing started, using flat irons
> which were heated up on the fire grate.[6]

Wash day was the same for working-class women across the
whole of Yorkshire, and the process didn't change until electric
washing machines were affordable, which for most wasn't until
after 1950. In 1928, Leeds Corporation opened a municipal
wash-house. There were two kinds of wash – the 'twopenny',
where women did the washing themselves, and the 'ninepenny',
where they could use a washing machine. The twopenny wash
proved more popular, not because it was cheaper, but because
the women were more accustomed to washing by hand, and
because they believed handwashing would get the clothes
cleaner. One woman spoke for many Yorkshire women when
she said how glad she was to use the wash-house, because
she hated to put worn or patched clothes on the line for the
neighbours to see, 'for there isn't a woman, poor or rich, who
hasn't her pride.'

Another woman's daughter said of the wash-house, 'Now
we'll be able to have all cleared up before dinner-time. Dad will
like that.'[7]

Even when women worked the same hours as their
husbands and fathers, the household chores still fell to them.
For generations, 'Dad' will have expected the women to have
cleaned the house and for his tea to be ready for him on the
table when he got back from work.

A mill girl said in the 1860s:

> On Saturday the mills close at midday and the men and
> single women make real holiday, but the married women

... are obliged then to set to work harder than ever. They have only this day to clean their houses, provide for the week's bake for the family, mend clothes, besides doing any washing that is not put out, and attend the market to purchase the Sunday's dinner ... so that the poor mother seldom gets a rest ere the Sabbath dawns if, indeed, she is not up all night.[8]

In 1857, Sir Francis Crossley opened the People's Park in Halifax. His aim was to have art and nature 'within the walk of every working man in Halifax; that he shall go to take his stroll there after he has done his hard day's toil.' At this time women outnumbered men in the textile industry in the town. There is

Investment (savings) leaflet 1920s (IMG/1451 Courtesy of Lloyds Banking Group plc Archives)

no mention of a place for them to stroll. It's likely they would have had no time.

Upper-class women would have a hierarchy of servants to do the household drudgery. Most middle-class households also had a servant, but with the never-ending nature of housework, the women and girls of the household would still have had to help. Mary Schroeder, whose father was a minister at Northgate End Chapel, recalls how in the early twentieth century her mother and the maid would work side-by-side in the kitchen. After washday, there was sewing and mending to be done. Everything was home-baked, and Friday was baking day. The range provided a valuable source of warmth in winter, but in the height of summer – in a tiny kitchen – one can only imagine how stifling a small kitchen in a terraced house must have been on baking day.

Fridges were not common until after 1950, and so shopping trips had to be done every couple of days. Saturday meant shopping for fruit and vegetables in the covered market, where women had to have keen mental arithmetic and negotiating skills as they sought out the best bargains.

'When plums or marrows were plentiful, we made jam. When blackberries were ripe, we gathered them for boiling. When eggs touched rock-bottom in the market, we bought them in quantity and pickled them in brine.'[9]

During both world wars, housewives were forced to show even more ingenuity in providing nourishing food for their families. Phyllis Bentley was disappointed that caring for her mother meant she wasn't able to take a more active role during the war, but she stated that:

> These months at home, living the ordinary life of the middle-aged provincial woman of the day, taught me how right Ernest Bevin was when he remarked that the women tipped the scales of victory… It was the ordinary housewife who was in fact decisive. She could have lost the war in any week. Struggling to feed and clothe her family – meat and milk and butter and cheese and

Savings advertisement 1955 (IMG/273 Courtesy of Lloyds Banking Group plc Archives)

margarine and tea and sugar and eggs and soap were rationed, clothes and sweets could only be bought by coupons – if she had once revolted, or cheated on a large scale, the whole system would have become unworkable. Starvation and rioting would have followed.[10]

The Ministry of Food set up a chain of British Restaurants in the Second World War to provide cheap, nourishing meals for those who needed it, but the bulk of the worry about feeding the family fell to women. An advertisement in the Second World War asked, 'Can a Warden Be a Good Wife?' In it, a husband comments on the fact that his dinner is cold again. His wife has been on warden duties all day. She wonders if it would be better to give up her post. God forbid her husband should have to cook his own meal after work. Luckily, Preen's Puddings provide ready meals. The wife is able to continue both saving the neighbourhood and providing hot dinners.

In fairness to the men of the time, they had been taught that cooking was women's work. As has been seen in the previous section, boys were excluded from lessons on domestic science and needlework. Whole generations of men were raised unable to cook a simple meal.

Vacuum cleaners, twin-tub washing machines and fridges were to remain luxury items until well after the Second World War. It is no surprise that until then, if they could afford not to take paid employment, many working-class women chose to stay at home in order to cope with the endless hours of housework.

Women queuing outside the British Restaurant, Heptonstall, 1940s (PHDA/ Community Collection HCC00607)

Courtship and Marriage

In the nineteenth century the reputation of middle- and upper-class women in society had to be immaculate. They were expected to have a complete lack of sexual experience before marriage, and even an ill-judged flirtation could mar a reputation irretrievably. Chaperoned as these girls were by their families, and educated apart from boys, in many cases they grew up genuinely sexually ignorant.

In 1823, Anne Lister received a gossipy letter from Mrs Norcliffe: 'What do you say of Captain Parry's match being broken off? The *true* reason is that the young lady formerly, when *very young*, it was thought, had a penchant for their groom or coachman.'

Captain Parry – later Rear Admiral Sir William Parry – was a celebrated Arctic explorer. According to Mrs Norcliffe, Parry was enough in love to overlook Miss Brown's teenage flirtation, but only, crucially, 'so long as it was not generally known'. Sadly for Miss Brown the gossips got to work, and when Captain Parry returned from his ship, 'finding it had been universally talked of, he declined the connexion'. Mrs Norcliffe goes on to say, 'It is rather *hard* on the young lady, who has behaved very well ever since they were contracted & had never deceived him... The errors of 15 might, I think, have been forgotten at, let us say, 25.'[11]

An article was circulated in the press stating that Captain Parry had 'met with a severe and unlooked for disappointment', which had caused him conflicting struggles between affection and duty, and that despite Miss Brown's 'sincerity of affection', the engagement was called off.[12]

We can't now know what Miss Brown's relationship with her groom was, but even if it was entirely innocent, once her name began to be bandied about in the press and the gossip began circulating, her reputation was sullied. Her marriage to Captain Parry never went ahead. As Mrs Norcliffe points out wryly in her letter, 'I presume he will be reserved for some Lady Mary or Lady Betty who, if no better than poor Miss Brown, will have title & blood to hide any failings.'

Miss Brown's social standing was not enough to ride the gossip. In 1826, Captain Parry married Isabella, daughter of Sir John Stanley, and went on to have ten children.

In many respects, working-class women had a lot more freedom than middle-class women like Miss Brown. Even if a working-class woman became pregnant outside marriage, it didn't mean no man would ever marry her. Trips were made to the altar with new-born babies, and men were known to marry women who had had an illegitimate child by another man. Mary Black, the mother of suffragette Lavena Saltonstall, had a 5-year-old illegitimate daughter when she married John Saltonstall in Halifax Parish Church in 1880.[13]

Before the 1870 and 1882 Married Women's Property Acts, and the Infant Custody Act of 1873, all married women, whatever their class, were subject by law to the following:

> A wife loses all her rights as a single woman, and her existence is entirely absorbed in that of her husband. He is civilly responsible for her acts... What was her personal property before marriage, such as money in hand, money at the bank, jewels, household goods, clothes, etc, becomes absolutely her husband's, and he may assign or dispose of them at his pleasure, whether he and his wife live together or not.

> The legal custody of children belongs to the father. During the lifetime of a sane father, the mother has no rights over her children, except a limited power over infants, and the father may take them from her and dispose of them as he thinks fit.[14]

It is almost impossible for us in the twenty-first century to understand just exactly what it must have been like to be a married woman in Halifax 200 years ago, but reading these marriage laws gives us some conception of the complete lack of power women had, and their complete subjection to men. We wonder these days why on earth a woman would marry given such terms, but for almost all women in the nineteenth century, marriage was an economic necessity. As has been seen in the chapter on education, women in the nineteenth century were barred from the professions. What jobs there were available to them were low-paid. Even working-class women who did the same job as men were usually paid less than their male counterparts, because it was taken for granted that women would marry and would therefore be supported by their husbands and didn't 'need' the extra money in their wage packet.

Middle- and upper-class women in particular, with no real opportunity of supporting themselves independently by taking a job such as factory work, were obliged either to rely on relatives or to marry. Anne Lister's lover, Isabella, worries about the fate of her sister, Charlotte. Isabella hints to Anne that perhaps Charlotte could come and live with them. When Anne appears reluctant, Isabella says, 'I cannot forsake my sister. Surely you would not wish it.'[15]

Marianne Belcombe was the love of Anne Lister's life. She married Charles Lawton for financial reasons, but even after marriage her future was still not secure. Lawton told Marianne that if she failed to produce an heir, he would leave her nothing in his will. Marianne was forced to rely on Anne Lister's generosity. Without her generous and forgiving lover, she could have ended up virtually penniless.

Marianne's husband's cruelty makes one wonder what else he subjected his wife to. But even if Marianne were living with a monster, she would have virtually no means of escape. Except in extremely rare cases a woman could not obtain a divorce, and in any case, filing for divorce cost money, and a wife's money belonged to her husband. Unless she had friends or family to support her, she was completely at her husband's mercy.

Until the 1857 Matrimonial Causes Act, divorce cases were heard before an Ecclesiastical Court. In 1855, the *Halifax Courier* reported on a case being heard in York. A Mrs Ackroyd of Knaresborough was filing for divorce on the grounds of her husband's cruelty. She was so fearful of violence, she had fled the home to stay with a friend. The court heard an account of the husband's threatening behaviour and of his stalking, including how he'd threatened his wife with razors, and how he'd ridden up to her friend's house and smashed a window with the butt of his whip. He then went to her father's shop and smashed glass there, being driven off eventually by neighbours armed with 'sticks, brush shafts, &c'. The husband 'persisted in this outrageous conduct for four hours ... followed as he rode up and down by hundreds of boys, he caused great fear to his wife, who was obliged to be removed to the back part of the house.'

Mrs Ackroyd's solicitor gave a spirited description of the effects of long-term intimidation on her state of mind, concluding that 'the conduct of the defendant produced in her a degree of alarm and excitement which was dangerous to her life.' The solicitor's speech was in vain. The chancellor presiding over the hearing replied:

> [Mrs Ackroyd] leaves her husband and then comes and pleads a great number of acts done by him which are offensive to her and to her relatives, who are countenancing the wife's voluntary withdrawal from her conjugal duties. Her primary duty is to consort with him and to bear and forebear. She withdraws herself and exasperates him… If there was any unpleasantness between Mrs Ackroyd and her husband, it was her duty to make the best and not the worst of it, in which case it was her duty to mitigate and not to aggravate the evil.[16]

Mrs Ackroyd is blamed for 'exasperating her husband' and provoking his 'unpleasantness', and for not 'mitigating' his evil. She now has no other recourse in law. Until 1891, if a wife ran away from a marriage, the police could capture and return her, and her husband could have her imprisoned.

After the 1857 Matrimonial Act, men could divorce their wives for adultery. Wives would have to prove adultery and another factor, such as incest or assault, before being granted a divorce. Some members of the working classes believed 'wife-selling' was a legal form of divorce. It's difficult to estimate how widespread the practice was in the nineteenth century, since only notorious or public cases of wife-selling reached the courts or the newspapers. According to some figures, the practice was more common in Yorkshire than anywhere else.[17]

In 1824, Anne Lister wrote in her diary:

> John Anderson used to tell me long since of wives being cried 3 market days at the market cross & sold the last day & 'livered (delivered) in a halter. He said Phoebe Buck, the leech-woman still living, I believe, at Market Weighton, was sold in this way & bought by Buck, the man she lived [with] ever after.[18]

To fit the terms of the ritual, wife-selling had to be done in a public place such as the market square, and the wife had to be put in a halter to be 'delivered'. The sale of the wife was almost always by mutual agreement, and although the sale took place in public, her new husband would already have been decided on.[19]

The practice of wife-selling appears to have continued well into the second half of the nineteenth century. In Thomas Hardy's *The Mayor of Casterbridge*, published in 1886, Michael Henchard sells his wife and daughter to a sailor.

Wife-selling was roundly condemned in the press, although they enjoyed making a meal of the stories. In 1838, *The Northern Star* reported:

> One of those occurrences of selling a wife, so disgraceful to civilized society, and especially to Englishmen, took place last week, in a village near Bradford. The name of the seller is J. Wilkinson, and that of the buyer James Ellison. The former, being tired of his spouse, agreed to sell her to the latter, whose wife had run away, for 1s. The bargain was struck in the presence of a witness, and the poor woman was hoisted away, bag and baggage, to the residence of the new lord. In the morning he heartlessly turned her out, and her husband refused to take her.[20]

Michael Henchard en route to sell his wife and child (Robert Barnes illustration 1886 Mayor of Casterbridge *serial)*

The passing of the Married Women's Property Act of 1870 gave women the right to earn or inherit their own money. As the main wage earners, however, men still controlled the household finances. There were many families where the husband drank the money away. Temperance Societies played an active role in many chapels in Halifax and surroundings and were strongly supported by women. The Band of Hope was an organisation for children, formed in Leeds in 1847, in an attempt to give an early education on the evils of drink.

Mary Schroeder recalled at the start of the twentieth century:

> Another vivid memory of Northgate End is of our
> Band of Hope... The pledge, in its day, did much to

uphold decent family life in Halifax. Wages were low, and if the wage earner, instead of pouring the whole of his week's wages in his wife's lap on Friday night, turned aside to fritter them away at the local pub, the whole family would suffer, for it was the housewife who had to put food on the table. The loss even of sixpence put her housekeeping out.[21]

The First World War brought huge social changes for women, many of whom entered the workplace for the first time. With the Representation of the People Act in 1918, the first women gained the vote. Not long afterwards, in 1923, new legislation placed men and women on an equal footing when petitioning for divorce on the grounds of adultery. In 1926, the legal age of marriage for girls, with their parents' consent, was raised from 12 to 16. In 1937, both wives and husbands could petition for divorce on the grounds of cruelty, desertion and insanity.

In 1950, most women left work on getting married. Looking after the family was seen as their 'job'. This work was unpaid, and they continued to be unequal in financial terms with men and to earn less in the workplace. By this time, however, women were better educated than in 1800, universities and most professions were open to them, and they had greater opportunities to earn their own income.

Sexual Abuse and Harassment

Establishing the extent of sexual abuse and harassment in the nineteenth and early twentieth century is impossible. If we think of the respected and successful men in the twenty-first century whose crimes remained hidden for decades, it's hard to believe that the few cases of abuse which came to court between 1800–1950 weren't the tip of an enormous iceberg. As this is a book about women's lives in Halifax, this section does not cover the abuse of boys. It must be noted, though, that sexual abuse of boys was barely reported at all. Uncovering any cases of abuse of boys in the nineteenth century is even more unlikely than discovering the extent of the abuse of women and girls.

Band of Hope demonstration (PHDA/Alice Longstaff Gallery Collection ALC01399)

The term 'sexual abuse' wasn't used widely until the 1980s. Rape claimants weren't given anonymity until 1976. Even with anonymity, women are still reluctant today to come forward to report rape, abuse or harassment. In the nineteenth century it was virtually impossible for middle- and upper-class women to come forward. For such a woman, even to have her name associated with a sexual crime would mean her reputation was tarnished. To make it harder for historical researchers, newspaper reports couched sexual offences in terms such as 'immorality' or else 'indecent assault', which could range from an attempted kiss to actual rape.

Anne Lister, who walked great miles alone around Halifax, recounts in her diaries several instances of being accosted:

> A man in a greatcoat made like a soldier's followed me down our lane & asked if I wanted a sweetheart. He was a few yards behind & I said: 'If you do not go about your business, sir, I'll send one that will help you.' I heard

him say, 'I should like to kiss you'... I felt, on coming upstairs, as if I could have knocked him down.[22]

This sort of verbal harassment is demoralising and frightening when it happens frequently, as it almost certainly did for women walking alone at that time. The next incident Lister records was more threatening:

> My usual way to King Cross & back & got home at 5½. About midway between the two sets of cottages in the new bank as I returned, a man, youngish & well enough dressed, suddenly attempted to put his hand up my things behind. In the scuffle I let my umbrella fall but instantly picked it up & was aiming a blow when the fellow ran off as fast as he could, & very fast it was. I did not feel in the least frightened, but indignant & enraged.[23]

Fortunately Lister was brave and angry enough to scare the man off. She didn't report the incident to the police. She didn't even consider telling them. Lister would have had to send someone to fetch a constable. She might then have felt embarrassed explaining to a male constable what had happened. Besides, the assailant had run off, and the probability of finding him again wasn't great. This type of incident was all too regular. Many women must have resigned themselves to the fact they could be subjected to assault if walking alone in broad daylight.

In 1853, a woman called Elizabeth Hargreaves actually did report an assault. She had been travelling by train from Halifax to Bradford. When the train passed through a tunnel and the carriage was plunged into darkness, she was assaulted by a fellow passenger. The man was drunk and she reported him to the railway staff at Low Moor, where the police were called. He was found guilty of 'indecent assault' and ordered to pay a fine or take a month's imprisonment.[24]

The term 'indecent assault' was vague, and covered a range of crimes. In February 1868, a painter was accused of 'indecent assault' of an 8-year-old girl who lived in George Street. The *Halifax Courier* reported that 'the particulars are quite unfit for publication'. The man was sentenced to six months.[25] Without knowing the full facts, it's hard to say what his sentence would have been today, but it seems likely a present-day court would have thought six months far too lenient a sentence.

Women had to be seen to be 'innocent victims', otherwise they were held to be partly responsible for the assault. In 1854, a man was charged with 'indecent assault' on a married woman at her home at Cross Fields, while her husband was at chapel. The case was heard behind closed doors and 'occupied the Court for a long period'. Again, the paper reported that 'the particulars are unfit for publication'. The man was found guilty but only given one month's imprisonment, because the woman had 'been in his company at a public house previous to the assault, and there was gin on the table before them'.[26]

Domestic servants were particularly vulnerable to abuse. They had often moved away from their families and might be the only servant in the house, with no one to turn to for help.

In the 1930s, Rita Humphreys travelled to Harrogate to meet the canon of the parish in which she would be working:

> On arrival I was ushered into a sitting-room by the canon's wife who then went off to make a cup of tea. I was left standing, facing the canon, who began to ask me about the job I was taking up at the Hydro Hotel. As I spoke the canon moved nearer to me and, as I talked, he put his hands on my shoulders. From there he proceeded to feel my neck and breasts. As his hands wandered downwards I was paralysed with fear and wondered what to do when, mercifully, his wife was heard approaching with a tray of tea and the canon broke away from me.[27]

Rita told her mother, who was working for a vicar at the time. Her mother told the vicar what had happened, but 'he did not believe it, so nothing was done'.

Women who worked in the mills and factories may have been better protected from harassment, since they worked in communities. However, although male mill workers' morals were rarely the subject of debate, much was made in the press of the 'immorality' of mill women.

In 1859, the National Association for the Promotion of Social Science met in Bradford. A paper, written by an anonymous 'lady', was read out to the meeting: 'The writer drew a fearfully dark picture of the evils resulting to females from the factory system... Among other startling assertions was that swearing was prevalent among them; that modesty was an exception, and indecency the rule.'[28]

One of the other speakers present hotly championed Yorkshire mill women, stating the writer hadn't painted an accurate picture. An 'interesting discussion' followed. However, the anonymous lady's views were widely held, and the question of mill women's immorality was even discussed in a government inquiry. In her report on the employment of women in 1892, Assistant Commissioner May Abraham stated:

> There is no special tendency to immorality among mill workers. Much of the good conduct of the mill depends upon the individual character of the [male] overlookers; and, in those mills where care is taken by the masters, the morality is necessarily better than in the mills where the masters set a low tone.[29]

Abraham added, 'there are undoubtedly some few cases of direct immorality in connexion with a system of "favouritism".'

Abraham does not elaborate on what this system of favouritism entailed. If systematic sexual harassment was taking place in certain mills, the whole subject is brushed aside in one sentence. She was far more troubled by the fact that often men and women had to share the same toilet facilities. This was seen by outsiders to the mill as a direct contribution to 'immorality'. The women themselves were probably far more concerned with the often disgusting and positively unhealthy state of the toilets.

Women in the Burling and Weaving Shed, John Oakes and Sons, Regent Works, Halifax 1896 (Courtesy of Steve Gee)

Some mills were better than others, and Crossley's Carpets employed (female) staff to keep the toilets clean.

The mill women could certainly give as good as they got on occasion. J. B. Priestley, who worked in Bradford before the First World War, recalled:

> It is true that the women and girls who worked in the mills then were no models of feminine refinement... It was still the custom in some mills for the women to seize a newly-arrived lad and 'sun' him, that is, pull his trousers down and reveal his genitals.

However, Priestley adds, 'There was nothing sly, nothing hypocritical about these coarse dames and screaming lasses, who were devoted to their own men.' He contrasts this with the 'cynical whoring' of mill masters, 'who were obdurate if the mill girls wanted another shilling a week [but who] could be found in distant pubs turning the prettiest and weakest of them into tarts.'[30]

Priestley used his experience of this 'cynical whoring' as part of his play, *An Inspector Calls*, set in 1912, in which a young woman in a manufacturing town commits suicide.

In 1939, the *Halifax Courier* reported that, 'The number of offences against women and children does not seem to diminish'. In the previous year there had been 'twenty-one cases of indecent assault on females'.[31]

Far from diminishing, this number was set to rise dramatically in the decades to follow, as women (and men) began to feel able to step forward and speak about their abuse.

Pregnancy and Childbirth

In 1924, when she was still at elementary school, Janet Cockcroft's favourite teacher died in childbirth:

> The funeral was a dreadful occasion... All the children were lined up outside school to see the silent procession go past. I had given my pennies to the wreath, and I wept. That was when I first determined that whatever I would do, it would be something to help women and to try to stop them dying in childbirth.[32]

The anticipation of going into labour often makes first-time mothers anxious, but in the nineteenth and early twentieth century, when death in childbirth was all too common, many pregnant women must have been terrified at the thought of the ordeal to come.

A typical cause of maternal death was excessive haemorrhaging. Janet Cockcroft remembered how her own mother suffered a colossal haemorrhage after the birth of her brother. The doctor asked young Janet to run out into the garden to fetch stones to prop up the end of the bed – a common rough-

and-ready practice to help stem the flow of blood. It's hard to imagine the terror in a household at such a time – at a time, too, when the family faces all the demands of a new-born baby.

Puerperal fever, or postpartum infection, was also common. Until the latter half of the nineteenth century many medical professionals refused to believe that infections such as septicaemia were transmitted by the very people giving care to the women in labour. Many deaths could have been prevented if doctors and midwives had understood the need for washing their hands before examining a patient. With our present-day antibiotics, and with our understanding of the need for hygiene, death from puerperal fever is now rare in the UK. In the years 1890–1900, at least fifty-seven women in Halifax died of an infection after giving birth. These figures were recorded by J. T. Neech, the Medical Officer of Health for Halifax, in his 1901 report. Some of these fifty-seven deaths may have been due to botched illegal abortions, but this is not noted by the MO.

Human stories tell us far more about what it was like to be a woman and pregnant in those times than statistics can. In the 1920s, Margaret Duffield, who lived in Boothtown, had a sister and sister-in-law, both of whom were pregnant at the same time. Duffield's sister, Betty, had already had one baby, but the birth had been traumatic. She had been advised not to become pregnant again. (Duffield doesn't record whether her sister was given any advice by her doctor on birth control.) Three years after the first baby, Betty fell pregnant again.

Duffield's sister-in-law, Cora, also pregnant, went into labour early. Both she and the baby died. The family tried to keep the terrible news from Betty until she'd safely delivered, but someone placed a notice about the deaths in the *Halifax Courier*. Duffield rushed over to her sister's house to try to prevent her reading the paper, but was too late:

> I found my sister sobbing on the settee and did my best to comfort her. It was a very unhappy time, as soon after that, on Whit Monday, Betty went into hospital to have her baby … but we lost her, too, and the new baby.[33]

Tales such as these and Janet Cockcroft's show far more clearly than numbers ever can the terrible tragedies involved in deaths in childbirth.

There was much discussion in Halifax at the turn of the twentieth century regarding the fall in population, and infant mortality was one of the areas of concern. J. T. Neech introduced a pioneering scheme of municipal health visiting to improve the welfare of pregnant women, nursing mothers and their babies. In 1908 he had leaflets distributed around the town advising on infant feeding, including the instruction that babies were not to be given 'fever powders, tea, wine or other spirituous liquors'.[34]

Also in 1908, the Mayor of Halifax introduced an extraordinary 'Baby Bounty' scheme. Under the scheme, the mothers of the first hundred babies born in the town that year, and registered with the Medical Officer, would receive £1 if the baby reached one year old. Ninety-one babies survived the year, and the Mayor handed out the sovereigns to the mothers at a special garden party.

He told them, 'I did not offer you this sovereign because you were poor. Nothing of the sort. I offered it purposely to encourage you to look after your babies for twelve months: for, if they are reared for the first year, the worst part is got over.'[35]

It's difficult to know how to comment on a scheme that rewards poor women with £1 if their babies haven't died after a year. At the very least it's worth pointing out how very distressing this must have been for those nine mothers grieving their own infants. Now, besides the sense of guilt they almost certainly already felt at 'allowing' their children to die, they had to stand aside and watch other mothers being rewarded. This assumption that poorer mothers were responsible for their children's deaths because they were careless and uneducated did nothing to address causes such as poverty, poor diet, poor sanitation and the overcrowding that bred disease.

Dr Alice Latchmore moved to Halifax during the First World War with her husband – a bank manager – and their two small children. Like Dr Cockcroft, Alice Latchmore had studied medicine at Edinburgh University. She attended the university in the very first year that women were accepted and was one of the first two women there to gain the degree of Doctor of Medicine.[36] Also like Dr Cockcroft, Dr Latchmore was particularly interested in child and maternal welfare. The rate of maternal mortality in Halifax was of grave concern at this time.

In his 1923 report, Cyril Banks, the then Medical Officer of Health for Halifax, wrote:

> The facts concerning Halifax have been discussed with Dr Janet Campbell, of the Ministry of Health, who has been making a special study of Maternal Mortality, and her report should be read by all who are interested in this important subject. The Halifax statistics quoted in the report make unpleasant reading.

Dr Latchmore was formally appointed by the corporation to run a Maternity and Child Welfare Centre in Northgate, along with similar centres on Queen's Road, Wade Street and Range Bank. Several weekly ante-natal clinics were set up around this time in the town, including one at the Halifax Royal Infirmary. These were also subsidised by the corporation. In addition to these clinics, Dr Latchmore also attended an ante-natal clinic run by the District Nursing Association on Clare Road. The nurses noted in their annual report of 1929–30: 'We trust [the clinic] will help to lessen the fears of child-birth, give confidence to the mother and help to reduce the maternal mortality which, unfortunately, in spite of all the care and precautions taken, remains almost stationary.'[37]

In the 1930s, Phyllis Bentley volunteered at Dr Latchmore's Range Bank clinic, which was held in a Sunday School. Bentley recounted how the district then,

> consisted of rows of small old smoke-blackened houses, with bad ventilation and no modern conveniences. Many of the women who brought their children were in extremely

1913 advertisement (Sunday School Week programme 1913, Calderdale Libraries)

poor circumstances, their husbands being engaged in low-paid unskilled labour; incipient anaemia showed in their pale gums; their hands were dirty and work-worn, their hair greasy, unwashed, often in curlers beneath their shawl... The children which these women unwrapped so tenderly were sometimes thin, sallow, fretful ... occasionally warped by a parent's venereal disease. [38]

The clinic sold orange juice and other children's food, but often the mothers couldn't afford it, even provided at wholesale prices.

Bentley writes of 'the signs of poverty, dirt, malnutrition and disease, and the keen suspense on the mothers' faces as they gazed at Dr Latchmore.'

Mayoress of Halifax Mrs Sharp discussing the value of orange juice. Welfare Foods Meeting in the Gas Showrooms (PHDA/Hebden Bridge Local History Society HLS01315)

The depression of the 1930s hit hard in Halifax, as it did in many towns and cities in the UK. Where food was short, mothers often bore the brunt of the hunger, serving the larger meal to the male wage earner and feeding herself after the children. The tenderness of the mothers witnessed by Bentley, and their poor physical health, is ample evidence that poor women in Halifax did not need a reward to take care of their infants.

Many factors contributed to falling maternal death rates from 1800–1950 – factors such as better understanding of hygiene, a rise in the standard of living for mothers, better ante-natal care, the introduction of antibiotics. The falling rate can't be attributed to one cause, but at the end of this period the MOH for Halifax was extremely happy to write in his report that, 'There were no maternal deaths in Halifax in 1951.'

Birth Control

In the nineteenth century, condoms weren't considered respectable by middle-class married women as they were associated with prostitutes; for poorer people, they were simply too expensive to buy on a regular basis. The diaphragm wasn't invented until the end of the nineteenth century, and again this was expensive and it had to be fitted by a doctor – and most doctors would consider birth control only where a woman was married and her health might be at risk with another pregnancy.

Becoming pregnant could be a complete catastrophe if a woman was unmarried and without the means to support herself. An unplanned pregnancy meant fear and shame. Pills of various dubious natures, promising to treat 'obstructions', 'abdominal complaints' and 'female irregularity', were widely advertised in magazines and newspapers well into the twentieth century.

Many women were prepared to take the most desperate measures. During the night of 18 December 1862, just a week before Christmas, 18-year-old Ann Chadwick gave birth to a baby girl while visiting her sister at her lodgings in Range Bank. The landlady, Mrs Tetley, had guessed Ann was pregnant when she'd arrived the day before, but Ann had denied it. We can only imagine the girl's terror as she gave birth during the night, with no medical assistance, trying to be as quiet as possible so as not to alert her suspicious landlady. The infant died – whether by natural causes or not isn't clear. Ann buried the body in the garden, where the inquisitive landlady found it the next day.

The story painted is one of desperation and tragedy. A surgeon was called to examine the dead infant. Ann was arrested and taken to the West Riding Police Court in Halifax, where she was sent for trial at York Assizes.[39]

In addition to the shame of the unwanted pregnancy, followed by a frightening labour, Ann faced the terror of a trial for a capital crime. She was unlikely to be convicted of murder, as most judges and juries saw young girls as innocent victims of seduction. However, the father is nowhere to be seen in this tragic tale and, as with many, many other women, Ann faced alone the consequences of their relationship.

Illegal abortion was an option for the desperate, right up until abortion became legal in 1967. The results of a backstreet abortion are movingly described by Halifax nurse Margaret Duffield. One evening during the 1940s, Duffield's friend arrived late at night. The friend was very ill. Duffield recalled:

> I said that I would fetch my doctor, but she became absolutely terrified and I realised this was no ordinary

EVERY WOMAN

Should send two stamps for our 32-page Illustrated Book, containing valuable information how all Irregularities and Obstructions may be entirely avoided or removed by simple means. Recommended by eminent Physicians, as the only Safe, Sure, and Genuine Remedy. Never Fails. Thousands of Testimonials. Established 1862. Mr. P. Blanchard, Walston-lane, London.   72

Todmorden Advertiser February 1908

illness; she was pregnant. I tried to prepare for what was to happen, as she begged me to help. She sobbed more than talked and, gripping my arm, fought through waves of terrible pain. She had become pregnant by an American soldier while her husband was abroad... A woman had performed [an abortion] only on the condition the girl left immediately and had the 'baby' elsewhere. She threatened to kill herself if I got the doctor, but I was in a dreadful situation myself. Who was this woman who had performed the abortion? And what had she done? My friend could die and taking part in this could be a criminal act. I had no answers to these questions and dilemmas, but my friend needed me badly and I had to get on with the job... Afterwards, strangely I thought at the time, she asked me what the baby was, and I said a boy. Dead now, of course. Later she went home, and I got busy getting rid of the evidence.[40]

When unmarried women went through with a pregnancy and kept the child, the stigma of the unplanned birth haunted them and the child for the rest of their lives. Rita Humphreys was born

John Hartleys Original Yorkshire Clock Almanack 1929

in the 1920s and grew up believing her father was dead. After Humphreys applied to join the WRENs, her mother got to the post first and threw away the navy's admission forms because she knew they would require a birth certificate. Humphreys believed the navy hadn't replied to her application and assumed they weren't interested. She applied to the RAF instead, and this time was able to fetch the mail in first. Her mother was finally forced to reveal the truth. Rita's father had been a teacher and was already married when they met. Her mother told her he had 'let her down, telling her she'd be all right.'[41]

Rita's mother felt all the social stigma of having a child outside marriage and was so ashamed she was prepared to let her daughter's career suffer. Once again the woman in the relationship took responsibility for the resulting child. Rita's father presumably earned a decent wage as a teacher, but Rita had grown up in appalling poverty, and her mother had looked after her alone.

St Margaret's House and the Moral Welfare Council

Many pregnant women were abandoned not just by the fathers of their children, but by their own families. Besides losing her job, a pregnant domestic servant could also lose the roof over her head.

There were several homes and refuges for unmarried or 'fallen' women in Halifax, but records of the women who stayed there are now almost non-existent, for obvious reasons. Many women did not want their pregnancy known. The Children's Homes website records a St Margaret's Hostel, or St Margaret's House, at St John's Lane in Halifax in 1908, which took in 'friendless and fallen girls'. There is no record of this hostel in the census of either 1901 or 1911. Records exist, however, for St Margaret's House in Balmoral Place, which took in unmarried mothers from at least the 1930s right up until the 1970s.

John Hartleys Original Yorkshire Clock Almanack 1929

St Margaret's House consisted of four terraced houses that had been converted into one. It was run by the rather forbiddingly named Halifax Rural Deanery Moral Welfare Council, which was part of the Church of England. The hostel relied at first on charitable donations, but in the late 1930s it began to run into debt. All sorts of fundraising activities were held. Staff of the hostel regularly gave talks at Mothers' Unions and in church halls; potato pie suppers and flag days were organised, and in 1949 tickets were sold to guess the length of a ball of wool, with the prize being a freehold cottage, generously offered by Alderman Holdsworth, the Mayor of Halifax. The cottage was won by Miss Grayson, a retired nurse of Moor End Road, who gave it back to be put up for auction to raise more funds.[42]

The stigma of unmarried motherhood presented a challenge to those wishing to raise funds for St Margaret's. Representatives of the Church of England were not always a help. In 1939, Canon James, the Vicar of Halifax, gave a speech to the Committee of Moral Welfare Work in which he said:

'The very nature of the work [of St Margaret's] itself forbade publicity. Many newspapers gave that side of life publicity, but he was glad to see that the "Halifax Courier and Guardian" did not.'[43]

Unable to give 'that side of life publicity', and with many people preferring to give money to causes which they thought were more worthy than that of 'fallen women', it's no wonder fundraisers struggled to raise money for the hostel.

In 1948, Halifax Council submitted its proposals for carrying out its duties under the new NHS Act. One of the proposals was to take over some of the costs of St Margaret's, as it was felt that, 'Hostel accommodation for unmarried mothers and their babies is necessary in the Borough.'[44]

In 1950, Halifax's Medical Officer of Health reported that the council was paying five-sixths of the running costs of St Margaret's.[45]

A lot has come to light in recent times about the way some homes for unmarried mothers were run in the twentieth century, with evidence showing many mothers in hostels were forced to give up their babies for adoption against their will. Homes such as St Margaret's, which were run by the Church of England's Moral Welfare Council, appear to have been far less repressive. However, Thea Skyte, who worked at St Monica's Home in Bradford – also run by the Church of England – recalled of her time there in the 1940s:

> At that time illegitimacy was looked upon as a sin and almost as a crime. The poor expectant mothers were strictly supervised, hardly allowed to go out, their incoming and outgoing mail restricted, opened, read and censored. They were allowed only very few visitors and male visitors were completely forbidden.[46]

Many women gave their babies up for adoption because they felt they had no choice, and many mothers never felt free to explore their options. This does not appear to have been the case at St Margaret's. In 1948, after the council took over part of the running of the hostel, Medical Officer of Health Dr Roe reported:

> The future security of the child has to be safeguarded as far as is possible, and the mother has to be helped to realise and enabled to carry out her responsibilities and this very often without any help from the baby's father. If advice and help can be given to an unmarried mother before the baby is born and afterwards, many foolish arrangements may be avoided and much suffering and unhappiness to the child may perhaps be prevented.[47]

Of the twenty-eight babies born at St Margaret's in 1948, only five were given up for adoption, and one was placed with a foster mother. Tragically, one baby died. The rest of the mothers elected to bring up their babies themselves, either alone, or with the help of their families or the father's family.

In 1950, Miss Westwood, a Moral Welfare Worker, wrote in that year's Medical Officer of Health's report:

> The mothers [at St Margaret's] stay with their babies on average for at least six weeks after being discharged from hospital. This period, short though it may be, means that the mother and child are together at the beginning and enables the mother to have some time to consider what is going to be the best future for the baby. The ideal of a child enjoying the natural right of being brought up by its own mother is unfortunately not always possible.

Miss Westwood adds poignantly, 'To many people it is surprising to see what care and love a single girl will give to her baby.'

St Margaret's House closed in the 1970s. Peter Harper, who bought the premises to convert into flats, recalled the beautiful grounds, 'perfect for pushing a perambulator around', and that the building, 'used to have a chapel, and some of the rooms were done out for use as a nursery with Snow White paintings on the walls.'

The same article in the *Halifax Courier* in 2007 states, 'It is easy to see how relaxing and carefree it must have been living here in the 1960s and 70s.'[48]

It's surprising how quickly the true situation for unmarried mothers has been forgotten. For the pregnant women at St Margaret's, with the weight of worry about their unborn child and their approaching labour, and with society regarding their pregnancy as shameful, life must have been anything but carefree and relaxing.

The Halifax Women's Welfare Clinic

In the early twentieth century, birth control was the subject of much heated debate. In 1922, the *Leeds Mercury* ran an article entitled, 'Is Birth Control Wicked?' The author discussed the 'doctrine' of birth control in terms of its effect on population. In a crowded city, birth control was understandable, he wrote, but in Australia, where birth control was apparently 'practised perhaps more extensively than anywhere else' (how the writer knew this is not recorded), the control of their fertility had made the Australian people 'probably the most selfish in the world'. The author adds, 'Where ... it is practised simply so that women can shirk the responsibilities and duties of life and have an easy time, nothing but evil and vice result.'[49]

Evil and vice are strong words indeed. Married women who wanted to control the number of children they had were stigmatised. Unmarried women who wanted to protect themselves from becoming pregnant were considered immoral for having sex before marriage.

Against this backdrop, in early 1934 an organiser from the National Birth Control Association approached Lady Fisher-Smith and asked her to suggest the names of women who would be interested in starting a family planning clinic in Halifax. A preliminary meeting was held, attended by ten women, where it was agreed to set up a Women's Welfare Clinic, with Dr Heynemann as the first Medical Officer and Miss Williamson as the first nurse, both unpaid volunteers. Money would be raised by public subscription, and patients would be asked to contribute towards the cost of their supplies. This first meeting was held on 2 February 1934. The women decided to approach Dr Roe, Halifax's then Medical Officer of Health, for premises for the clinic.

Three weeks later, on 23 February 1934, an announcement appeared in the *Leeds Mercury* stating that Dr Roe had himself begun a system of referring women to a birth control clinic. His clinic would be run by Dr Latchmore at the Northgate Maternity and Child Welfare Centre.[50]

Dr Roe was against the idea on principle of widening birth control to women who wanted to limit their families. His clinic would be strictly confined to married women who were referred by their medical adviser and whose lives might be at risk if they fell pregnant. It seems once Roe heard about the independent Women's Welfare Clinic, he wanted to take some control over the provision of birth control in Halifax.

Dr Janet Cockcroft, who took over from Dr Heynemann at the Women's Welfare Clinic (WWC) in 1950, recorded wryly in her memoir that Dr Roe had been 'unable' to provide the women with premises when they asked for help. TOC H, a charity for ex-servicemen, allowed the women to use their rooms at 32 Clare Road[51], but the use put to the room was controversial and the lease was soon terminated. This cost the WWC a fair amount of much-needed money, since equipment and furnishings had to be moved and new advertising material prepared. The birth control clinic eventually found a home in the Halifax District Nursing Association premises.

One of the first acts of the WWC was to send a letter to Halifax doctors, drawing their attention to the service: 'As the Local Authority is not yet permitted to give information on Birth Control except in cases where another pregnancy would be seriously detrimental to health, we have opened a voluntary clinic... A married woman doctor examines ladies with a trained nurse in attendance.'

The women also resolved to send the following letter to the Minister of Health, Ian Gledhill MP, and the town clerk:

> We, the Halifax Women's Welfare Clinic, welcome the advance … that the powers conferred by the Public Health Acts on Local Authorities permit of birth control advice being given at suitable clinics to all married women to whom pregnancy would be detrimental to health. In view of the serious figures of maternal mortality, 5.04 per 1,000 births in this town, one of the highest rates in the country, we call on all Local Authorities to make immediate use of these powers.

> We nevertheless maintain that in order to mitigate the evils of poverty, overcrowding, and as an alternative to much self-induced or attempted abortion, such advice should be readily available through the Public Health Service to every married woman who needs it.[53]

Dr Roe continued to withhold his support. Unable to advertise their services widely at the risk of offending public sensibilities, the women were obliged to exercise incredible tact in order to let women know of the clinic's existence.

The minutes of 11 March 1936 state: 'After a good deal of discussion it was decided not to hold a Public Meeting for the poorer class of woman. It was felt it might jeopardise our lease of rooms.'

The women of the clinic continued to try to work with Dr Roe, but relations were strained. They heard that he'd given a woman in Hebden Bridge the address of the WWC, but that he'd left her with the impression, 'it was a place of doubtful character'.[53]

The fact that Halifax's health official disapproved of the WWC must have made it even more difficult for local women to approach the new clinic. However, the staff of the WWC continued to persevere with Dr Roe, inviting him for lunch to meet them. They also gained vital support from the *Halifax Courier*, who agreed to advertise their opening times. Miriam Lightowler, Halifax's first female mayor, was also a supporter. Gradually, the clinic built up a successful patient list.

In 1936, Dr Roe's birth control clinic at the Maternity and Child Welfare Clinic closed. In Dr Roe's report of that year as Medical Officer of Health, he makes the terse comment: 'Since the Voluntary Clinic commenced to operate in the town the Municipal Clinic has practically ceased to function.'

Miriam Lightowler told the staff of the WWC that Dr Roe's clinic had closed because of, 'a deputation from the Catholics',[54] but the women were not convinced. In fact the Local Authority clinic had had few referrals from the start. In 1934 there were only forty-four referrals and in 1935 there were only thirty-two.[55] The independent Women's Welfare Clinic was simply more successful. The women of the WWC made efforts to go out into the community and educate women. Mrs Ramsden, for example, gave a talk on birth control to the Parent–Teacher Association at Battinson Rd School in 1937.[56] Efforts such as these brought the WWC to women's attention and helped

Dr Cockcroft in her maternity clinic (Photo courtesy of Philip Cockcroft and PHDA)

change the perception that this type of clinic was somehow 'dubious'.

In 1939, the Women's Welfare Clinic was finally recognised by the West Riding County Council Public Health Department, who began sending patients there and taking responsibility for their expenses.

Dr Janet Cockcroft later took over from Dr Heynemann. She recalled in her memoir how the clinic offered her 'a unique opportunity to help large numbers of women plan their pregnancies, safeguard their health and promote happy family life.'[57]

This must have been enormously satisfying and rewarding to Dr Cockcroft, who had determined to work in the field of women's health ever since witnessing the death of her beloved teacher when she was a child.

CHAPTER FOUR

Women in Employment

What Did Middle-Class Women Do?

According to some figures, before the First World War as many as six out of seven people in Britain left school at 14 to go to work.[1] In proportion to the number of working people, the number of middle- and upper-class women in Britain was small. Halifax was a town of working people in the nineteenth century and numbered even fewer middle-class women than the rest of the country. However, these few women were better educated and better able to leave a written record of themselves.

Anne Lister left a remarkably frank and detailed account of her life and of the lives of the women in her social circle in the first half of the nineteenth century. Although Lister had been well educated, when she left school all opportunities for a career were closed to her. Women of her day were excluded from university, law or medical school, from politics (except as unpaid canvassers), from taking a position in the church or the military. Society expected middle-class women like Lister to marry, and for their husbands to control the income. It was frowned on for women of her class to earn any type of living unless as a governess – and that was a last resort reserved for those women who had no husband or family to support them.

With no real opportunity of supporting themselves, unmarried middle-class women were forced to throw themselves on the mercy of their families, often moving around their various brothers and married sisters, where they faced being treated as unpaid help in the home. Marriage was an escape from this fate.

Despite being passionately in love with Anne Lister, Marianne Belcombe married Charles Lawton. Lister was deeply hurt, but she understood Belcombe's motives. She later said, 'If I could have allowed her twenty or thirty pounds a year in addition to what she had, she certainly would not have married. But what could she do on her allowance of only thirty pounds a year?'[2]

By the end of the nineteenth century, the situation for middle-class women had barely changed. In 1899, when the International Congress of Women met in London, *The Pall Mall Gazette* reported that one of the areas under discussion was 'the professions open to women … journalism, nursing, and inspectorships [of factories]'.[3] There are only three professions listed – and the field is even narrower when you take into account that women's 'journalism' meant writing about household matters, and that at the time there were only six female factory inspectors in the entire country.

In short, many middle-class women in Halifax in the nineteenth century had absolutely nothing to occupy their time. In 1832, Dr Belcombe diagnosed Anne Lister's lover, Ann Walker: 'Nothing the matter with her but nervousness. If all her fortune could fly away and she had to work for her living, she would do well.'[4]

Cooped up as she was at home, with nothing to occupy her except a few genteel hobbies such as music and needlework, we can understand how the daily boredom and a feeling of uselessness must have had a crippling effect on Walker's mental health.

For someone as energetic and active as Anne Lister – indeed, for any woman – the hours of enforced idleness must have been thoroughly depressing. Lister writes in her diary:

> Visiting hereabouts gives me no satisfaction & wasting my time in bed in a morning disturbs my happiness for the day. My only pleasure is in the thought of having employed myself profitably &, deprived of this, my spirits are unable to support themselves. I have felt low … all the day.[5]

Social engagements with the likes of the Misses Staveley and the Misses Greenwood – 'her mother as vulgar as ever'[6] – must have been a form of torture to Lister, who burned to be active and to employ her intelligence. Fortunately for her, she went on to inherit the estate and mines at Shibden Hall, and this gave her plenty to exercise her mind. But because Lister took charge of affairs herself, rather than leaving everything in the hands of an agent – and because she refused to marry and leave her affairs to a husband – she was treated as an oddity. Although she was resilient and had great strength of character, it's not surprising she often talks in her diaries of feeling low in spirits.

As already noted, over the period 1800–1950 educational opportunities for women increased. The attitude to middle-class women going out to work, however, changed little as the twentieth century began.

Halifax author Phyllis Bentley wrote in 1912 that, 'it was "not done" for a girl of a family like ours, in Halifax at any rate, to take paid work.' Bentley had left Halifax Girls' High School to go on to Cheltenham Ladies' College, where she had taken an external degree from London University. She was an academic, but girls were educated to become wives, or, in Bentley's case, 'to be a good daughter to my parents … less interested in books, more feminine, more sociable, more daughterly.'[7]

Like thousands of other women, Bentley gained a taste of independence during the First World War. She worked at the Ministry for Munitions in London, and for the first time she felt her life had meaningful value. When peace was signed, however, Bentley said that all of a sudden, 'it became the duty of all women to clear out … and leave the jobs open for the returning men.'[8]

Women were once again reduced to a sense of powerlessness. Bentley goes on to say that not long after the war: 'a headline in one of the popular newspapers announced stridently: A MILLION SURPLUS WOMEN. Surplus! Rather a bitter word. The reason for the surplus was even more bitter: a million dead men. Still, it was depressing to think we had no value save as mates.'[9]

Phyllis Bentley in 1957 (Calderdale Libraries)

The term 'surplus women' was coined in 1851, after the census of that year asked for marital status for the first time. The figures revealed that there were two-and-a-half million single women in the country. This caused an uproar, and single middle-class women were seen as a 'problem'.

In 1869, William Greg wrote an essay called *Why Are Women Redundant?* He maintained that working-class single women who were employed as domestic servants, 'are in no sense redundant … they fulfil both essentials of woman's being; they are supported by, and they minister to, men.'

According to Greg, single middle-class women, on the other hand, had no function except to marry. Many men at the time failed to share his view and many spoke up loudly in support of women, maintaining that there were, 'various interested motives that make men wish to keep women poor and desire them to be dependent.'[10]

More than half a century after unmarried middle-class women were first referred to as 'surplus' nothing had changed, and women as educated and intelligent as Phyllis Bentley were still having to state: 'I felt fiercely that women should have the right to work, the right to earn, for only so could they become independent, only so could they become free.'[11]

With two maids in the kitchen, there wasn't even any need for Bentley to help with the domestic chores: 'I accompanied my mother to town on domestic shopping expeditions, went "calling" with her and assisted her to receive her friends on the afternoon of the first Thursday in the month.' Not surprisingly, Bentley describes all this as 'blank, dreary, lonely, hopeless'.[12]

After Bentley's father died, her writing became a necessity to support her mother, and she finally felt a sense of purpose. She wrote poignantly,

> The cause of this necessity was a grief, but the work itself was not a grief to me. No woman today, thank goodness, will know the exquisite joy it gave me to earn... Today for a woman to earn and contribute is a commonplace. For me, at last it had become a duty to do what I most wanted to do in life.[13]

Dr Janet Cockcroft's battle to study medicine in the 1920s has been noted in the section on education. After graduating, in order for her to take up her chosen specialisation of obstetrics – the career she'd dreamed of since she was a child – Cockcroft had first to complete six months in surgery. Six weeks before her surgery stint was up, when she was about to take up 'her true career', war broke out. Every qualified woman doctor received a request from the government urging them to go into general practice, so that male GPs could go to war. Dr Cockcroft would have loved to have joined the Royal Army Medical Corps along with the men, but this was not allowed. Instead, she took up a position as a GP's assistant, which she described as 'all very pleasant, but a terrible anti-climax'.[14]

After the war, Janet Cockcroft took up a post at the Family Planning Clinic in Halifax. She continued to face prejudice, both for her choice of career and for going out to work:

> Socially, I was ostracised. No one wanted to know me. A conversation I had at one awful cocktail party was typical of the attitudes I met. A councillor condescended, 'Whatever do you want to work in a Family Planning Clinic for? It's a private thing, and people ought to look after that sort of thing by themselves. You've got a home and a child to look after. That should be your job'... I was even more annoyed to discover women were just as bad. They made it quite clear I should not work if Peter was able to support me.[15]

Women's Voluntary Work and Civic Influence

Middle-class women in Halifax faced barriers to taking up paid employment throughout this period, but the work they did on a voluntary basis made a vital and lasting difference. We've already seen how the Yorkshire Ladies Council of Education, which included Halifax women Mrs Crossley and Mrs Whitley, was instrumental in establishing Halifax High School for Girls. From early subscribers to the Infirmary, to teachers at Sunday Schools, to the running of Darby and Joan clubs and the Women's Royal Voluntary Service – the list of Halifax women's voluntary organisations and their activities from 1800–1950 is enormous.

Throughout the nineteenth century, bazaars selling 'fancywork' and crafts were a fashionable way for women to raise money, and many bazaars held in Halifax raised vast sums. The women responsible had exceptional organisational, networking and sales skills.

A bazaar to raise money for a new school and church at Queenshead (Queensbury) was held in April 1847 at the Assembly Rooms on Harrison Road. Persuading a titled guest to appear at a bazaar was a coup, and the ladies of Halifax managed to rope in no less a person than the Dowager Queen Adelaide. Lady Wharncliffe, Lady Mary Wood 'and other influential ladies of Halifax' were also present. Prominent women, including Mrs Akroyd, collected contributions of, 'Work or Materials, Game, Fruit, Wine, Confectionery, &c' to sell on their stalls. The bazaar was run over four days, with tickets going at two shillings apiece. The organisers were seeking to raise the astonishing sum of £600 (more than £50,000 in today's money).[16]

A bazaar at High Street Chapel in 1851, also attended by Mrs Akroyd and organised by Halifax women, raised the sum of £148. Even a conservative estimate would put this at over £15,000 today. The bazaar attracted an enormous crowd and the rooms were packed to the doors, but such was the women's organisational ability that despite the numbers, 'the arrangements were of the most orderly character, and prevented anything like confusion'.[17]

Although they had no vote, through many behind-the-scenes activities, middle-class women were also able to play a role in the political and civic life of the town. In 1820, when George IV was attempting to divorce Queen Caroline, the women of Halifax wrote a public letter in her support, which was published in the *Leeds Mercury*. The queen replied that she was 'far from being indifferent to the approbation of the Females of Halifax.'[18]

In 1905, the Halifax Citizens' Guild was formed in an attempt to make social initiatives more coordinated. Women numbered around half the membership of the Guild. In its early days, the Guild was responsible for projects such as encouraging people

BAZAAR.

QUEEN'S HEAD CHURCH AND SCHOOL.

LADY PATRONESSES.

Her Majesty Adelaide the Queen Dowager.
Lady Wharncliffe, Wortley Hall.
Lady Mary Wood, Hickleton.
Mrs. Wm. Haigh, The Shay.
Mrs. Geo. T. Pollard, Stannary Hall.
Mrs. Stocks, Catherine House.
Mrs. Edward Akroyd, Bank Field.
Mrs. Brooke, Birks Hall.
Mrs. Lancashire, Birks Hall.
Mrs. Bernard Hartley, Allangate.
Mrs. John Haigh, Savile Hall.
Mrs. Jer. S. Brown, West Field.
Mrs. Wm. Alexander, Carlton Place.

A BAZAAR, for the purpose of raising the requisite sum for paying off the balance remaining a charge upon the Building Committee of the above Church, and in aid of the Funds required for the ERECTION of a SCHOOL and SCHOOL HOUSE, upon an eligible Site given by GEORGE BARON, Esq. of South Cave, for that purpose, will be held at the Assembly Rooms, in Harrison Road, Halifax, on *Tuesday, the 6th of April*, 1847, and on the three following days.

Advertisement in the Bradford Observer April 1st 1847

to grow their own food on allotments, helping with the provision of free school meals, and the establishment of a maternity club called 'Babies Welcome', offering classes and maternity bags. The Guild later merged with the Halifax Council of Social Welfare.[19]

In 1907, women were allowed for the first time to stand for the local council, giving them their first opportunity to step out from behind the scenes and into government. In November 1918, the Halifax Council of Women Workers (later the National Council of Women) held its inaugural meeting. A year later, two of its members stood for the Town Council. The women were not successful. It wasn't until 1924 that Miriam Lightowler, chairman of the Poor Law Guardians, became the first woman councillor in Halifax. Mrs Lightowler went on to become Halifax's first female mayor in 1934.

Dr Janet Cockcroft was a leading light in the National Council of Women for many years from the 1930s. She later wrote about how the NCW provided an ideal training ground for women:

> It taught me confidence to speak in public and the ability to hold office. … The NCW is not a very large body but very influential, with high standards of debating, thinking and writing. Those members of the Halifax branch were a stern group of ladies, many of them real battleaxes, but they made me develop a social conscience about not only what was going on in this country, but round the world, too. I became extremely well-informed and learned to hold my corner in discussion with other women and men.[20]

Dr Cockcroft went on to use the NCW as a platform to fight for women's health issues and became president of the organisation in the 1970s.

Even after Miriam Lightowler successfully stood in the municipal elections, women in Halifax still seemed reluctant to put themselves forward. It must have been extremely hard for middle-class women, who had never had paid employment, to step out of the home and become the first female in a male-dominated sphere – a sphere which also required speaking in public. Voluntary work could be done in their own time and was easier to combine with all the many chores involved in looking after a house and family. It may be, too, that some of the women's husbands might not have been happy to have their wives working, and possibly entering a sphere above their own.

Some observers have attributed the lack of working-class female candidates in Halifax to women's subordinate role in the textile industry, where, although women formed the majority of the workforce, they were confined to lower-paid work.[21] But if the middle-class women of Halifax were apprehensive about stepping forward, or felt that they were unable to leave their commitments in the home, it seems even less likely that working-class women would come forward to do so. Miriam Lightowler had been to grammar school and was married to a businessman who was a Conservative councillor. She already mixed in the right circles. Most working-class women in the early twentieth century would have left school as soon as possible to start work. It would have taken someone of supreme confidence to step into a role that is perceived to be for the educated, and for educated men, at that.

In 1939, Miriam Lightowler gave a talk to the Halifax Business and Professional Women's Club, asking them to consider joining the council. She attempted to persuade them by outlining areas 'suitable for women', such as Health, Public Assistance and the Housing Committee.[22]

The Housing Committee at Halifax Council was certainly thought to lack enough women on board. Many communities in the thirties were being broken up, with houses in areas such as Haley Hill and the former Dobby Hall being demolished and families moving to new estates at Ovenden, Pye Nest and Pellon. At a meeting of the Halifax Drapers' and Hosiers' Association at the White Swan in Halifax in March 1939, the council was criticised for not taking working women's needs into consideration when designing the estates. Association member

Mrs Marsland claimed women in the new estates would now have to pay for a bus in order to do their shopping, and that the houses had nowhere to dry washing. She said, 'had there been more women on the Housing Committee, there would have been a far more practical municipal house today.'[23]

The Beacon Club was an organisation run by women volunteers to help young people in Halifax. Around this time the organisers recognised the needs of teenagers on the new estates, and the difficulty they found forming new friendships after their old communities were gone. The club ran activities which were lively and well attended and gave the young people a sense of themselves in their new surroundings. One woman later said that volunteering for the Beacon Club had made her realise, 'what a great force women were and could be.'[24]

As Janet Cockcroft later wrote about her time with the NCW, volunteering and organising charity work is a great training ground for public life. Gradually, more and more women in Halifax began to come forward. In 1939, of the fifteen new Justices of the Peace for Halifax Borough, a third were women. These women had all started out by playing important roles in voluntary organisations in the town – organisations such as the Beacon Club, the Electrical Association for Women, and the Women's Gas Development Association.

In the 1940s, Halifax volunteer group the Standing Conference of Women's Organisations, established in 1942, made a concerted effort to get women into influential positions. The SCWO created a panel of women suitable for appointment to council committees, hospital boards and the magistracy. However, the council refused to allow the women onto the Housing Committee and would only accept them if they were formally elected. They urged the women who had come forward to put pressure on political parties to select them as formal candidates. No political parties appeared willing to adopt them, so the women of the SCWO put two women forward as independent candidates of their own. One of these candidates was immediately taken on by the Liberal Party. On 3 November 1945, the SCWO paid for an advertisement in the *Halifax Courier*, urging women to vote for their women candidates, 'as far as their consciences allowed'. Both the women were elected. Afterwards, the Conservative Party asked the SCWO to suggest a suitable candidate to stand for them in a forthcoming by-election.[25]

During the 1930s and 40s the *Halifax Courier* ran a column called 'The Woman's Sphere', which regularly reported on all the Halifax women's organisations. The social circle for middle-class women in Halifax was relatively small, and many of the same faces appeared at different charity meetings in the Mikado Café on Commercial Street. These meetings were a chance for women to socialise as well as organise, and it wasn't unusual for their gatherings to involve 'jolly games', with prizes such as, 'such useful articles as a card of linen buttons and a potato knife'.[26]

Halifax's branch of the National Council of Women was responsible for establishing the Women's Voluntary Service in the town. Although the Second World War was said to be a great social leveller, in general voluntary work in Halifax continued to be mainly the preserve of the middle classes until long after the war had finished. One post-war volunteer for the WVS recalls that when she joined the Halifax branch in 1965, 'it was mostly upper-middle-class ladies who volunteered, but this gradually changed to mill workers and more working-class people.'[27]

Over this long period, voluntary work provided middle-class women in Halifax with a sense of fulfilment, an opportunity to take the lead in social initiatives, and an opportunity to take part in politics – at first behind the scenes, and then gradually by stepping in when civic roles were eventually open to them. In 1945, Phyllis Bentley told a meeting of the Leeds Women's Luncheon Club, 'Women must take their place in public and civil life.'[28] Voluntary organisations were an excellent starting point for women to enter into civic roles when they were finally permitted to stand for them.

Working-Class Women and Their Jobs

Working women in Halifax were employed in a vast range of jobs, both formally and informally. Laundresses, childminders, waitresses, landladies, tailors and dressmakers, shopkeepers, publicans, cleaners, saddle-makers, milliners, market-stall holders, servants of all descriptions, factory and mill workers, nurses, midwives – in Halifax, the so-called 'town of a hundred trades', the list is long. There is even a female 'wharfinger' or harbourmaster listed in White's Directory of 1837, living at 20 Old Cock Yard.

Unfortunately censuses in the nineteenth century don't provide an accurate record of women's employment. For most of this century, only the occupation of the head of the household – usually male – was recorded. But women's wages – and before 1918 the children's wages, too – were vital in almost every working-class household. Even so, attitudes to working-class women going out to work, just as for middle-class women, were often negative. These attitudes varied depending on the economy. When times were hard, working women were seen as 'taking the men's jobs' and undercutting men's wages because they were paid less. Women were also seen as neglecting their families by working – even when they were working precisely because their families needed the money they brought in. In fact, far from neglecting their children, most working-class women had arrangements within their communities for the care of their infants, either at dame schools, or with family, or with neighbours. In the nineteenth century their children often joined them in the mills at a young age.

Even in 1939, after all women were eligible to vote, and women in Halifax were beginning to stand for public office, Canon James, the Vicar of Halifax, told a meeting of the Halifax Round Table, 'It is an evil that women can earn and men can't. Woman has attained an economic independence which she hates to give up. Surely it is wrong.'[29]

Where they had to go out to work, women were as conflicted about whether they were neglecting their families as the men. As Dr Janet Cockcroft noted, there were many women as well as men who were adamant that mothers should not work at all. Margaret Duffield, who was born at the turn of the twentieth century, wrote in her memoir, 'Stop telling mothers about how to avoid being mothers, or about how they can be a part-time worker, or even a full-time worker and a mother, taking shortcuts with the most important job in the world, teaching, caring, nursing ... babies, children and [the] youth of the world.'[30]

The Sex Disqualification (Removal) Act of 1919 made it illegal to exclude women from jobs because of their gender. Doors to professions previously closed to educated women were beginning to open, but the question of whether married women – and particularly mothers – should work outside the home continued to be a cause of much debate. In the 1950s, Halifax nurse Mary Sykes applied to Leeds University to take a course in Health Visiting. She was asked to write an essay on the topic, 'The married woman who goes out to work is a curse to modern civilisation'.

Mary Sykes's reply was, 'I did not think she should work while the children were of pre-school age and then only part-time so as to be available when the children came home from school.'[31]

At times of economic necessity, attitudes were different. One Halifax mother recalls that during the Second World War,

> I used to take my baby son to a nursery on my way to work and pick him up again at tea-time, there was no problem getting children into nurseries, in fact the government were encouraging it, so that they could get as many women out to work as possible. There was none of this about working mothers having a bad effect on children's development – they were actually telling us it was good for them.[32]

Many schools in Halifax began to offer school dinners during the war, too, so that mothers would find it easier to take up the posts vacated by the men who had joined up.

After the war, at a time when women textile workers were desperately needed in the mills, voluntary organisations run by the middle-class women of Halifax also made efforts to help working-class women stay in the workplace. In 1948, the Halifax

Standing Conference of Women's Organisations organised a week's camping at Jerusalem Farm in the Luddenden Valley for 130 children, so that their mothers could continue to work during the school holidays.[33]

The divide between middle-class women (whose wage was not vital to their household's budget) and working-class women was often particularly in evidence when it came to the attitude towards working mothers. In 1948, the Soroptimists' International Convention in Harrogate discussed child welfare (by which they meant the welfare of working-class children), and although it was agreed that these children were fitter after rationing, Miss Elizabeth Hawes stated that, 'with their parents working they missed companionship and authority'. By 'parents', Miss Hawes meant 'mothers'.[34]

Although attitudes to their going out to work were almost always negative, working-class women played a vital part in the economic growth of Halifax. The following section will concentrate on three key employment areas for working-class women in Halifax from 1800–1950: domestic service, work in the factories and textile mills, and clerical work (focusing on the Halifax Building Society).

Women in Domestic Service

As we have seen, census returns in the nineteenth century don't give an accurate picture of how women were employed. The census didn't provide information on individual occupations until 1841, but even then enumerators were told, 'The professions &c. of wives … need not be inserted'. We do know that at the start of the nineteenth century many more women worked as domestic servants than men, and that in 1901, domestic service was still the largest employer of women in Halifax after the textile and clothing industry.[35]

The type of work done by female servants ranged in strict hierarchical order from housekeeper, cook, lady's maid, housemaid to kitchen or scullery maid, and, in larger households, various positions in between. Male servants such as butlers and footmen were seen as a luxury and were taxed from 1777 right up until 1937. An attempt was made to tax female servants in 1785, but this met with such protest the tax was halted after seven years.[36] Female servants were seen as a necessity, and indeed they played a vital role, contributing to the smooth running of the household and the happiness and harmony of their families.

Conditions for domestic servants varied enormously from employer to employer, from being isolated and abused, to being regarded as trusted and loved companions.

Eliza Oldham was a domestic servant in Rochdale and Halifax from the 1840s to the 1870s. In 1846, then in her twenties, she left her home, and her job at the cotton mill where she'd worked since childhood, to 'live in' as a general maid with Margaret Wood. A young woman would have thought hard about leaving the security of her job and family to go alone to a new establishment, but the families knew each other well. Eliza's father had previously worked for Margaret Wood's nephew, John Bright, the Quaker and radical Member of Parliament.

Eliza went on to develop a close and affectionate relationship with John Bright's daughter, Helen Clark. Such a loving friendship across classes was unusual. In their case it may have been easier to cross the barriers because John Bright had started from humble beginnings. Although Helen and Eliza were worlds apart socially, they wrote to each other for decades. Eliza once told Helen,

'I have often thought that if I lost your love it wd allmost kill me.'[37]

It's a revealing sentence and shows just how dependent Eliza was on the relationship. Helen Clark valued her Eliza's love and friendship greatly – enough to preserve her letters – and she did a great deal to support her in her old age, but she wasn't dependent on her. The difference in their stations can be seen when, in 1866, Helen married and moved to live in Somerset with her husband. Eliza, too, received a proposal of marriage. Female servants were generally expected to leave their jobs on marrying and, unlike Helen, Eliza was forced to choose between leaving her employment – where she said she had a good home – and taking a husband. Despite the fact the man was of good social standing, she turned him down.

In her old age, Eliza was lonely. She relied on Helen Clark's photos and letters, saying they did her good.

Phoebe Beatson was born in Halifax at the end of the eighteenth century. She worked as housemaid for an Anglican vicar, John Murgatroyd, in Slaithwaite, as well as taking in worsted spinning outwork from a wool-comber who lived in Holywell Green. John Murgatroyd's diaries survive, and his extraordinary and touching relationship with Phoebe has been brought to life in Carolyn Steedman's book, *Master and Servant: Love and Labour in the English Industrial Age.*

John Murgatroyd looked after Phoebe as he would a daughter – walking with her to the wool-comber's to show her the way, and walking with her again the next day because she is afraid of the bulls she has to pass on the way. In 1801, Phoebe fell pregnant to a local labourer, George Thorp. Murgatroyd urged Phoebe to marry, but when he took her to meet with Thorp, the man absolutely refused. Many clergymen of the time might have turned Phoebe out of the house. Instead, Murgatroyd helped Phoebe navigate the trauma and shame of having to go to the parish and name the father. The parish officers applied to the law for a 'bastardy order', and a warrant was served on Thorp for maintenance of his child.

Phoebe's baby, Elizabeth, was born in John Murgatroyd's house in 1802. The clergyman doted on the illegitimate child and talked of his household as a family. When he died in 1806 he left Phoebe the enormous sum of £150, and a further £150 for her daughter.

Although Murgatroyd's care for Phoebe is touching, their relationship was divided by their positions as employer and servant and by their class. Murgatroyd doesn't seem to have helped or expected Phoebe to learn to read, for example. When she finally married a John Sykes in Halifax, three months after Murgatroyd's death, she signed her name with an 'X'.

Living in with a family created a close and intimate relationship. Choosing a servant was an important decision, and many women relied on their social circle and family for recommendations. This meant, however, that once a servant had lost her reputation in a circle of possible employers, whether she was innocent or not, she would find it extremely difficult to get another position. When Mrs Norcliffe asks Anne Lister's advice regarding a servant, Anne strongly advises her against taking the woman on: 'The woman was turned off for giving away great quantities of bread & meat & will not do for Mrs Norcliffe at all.'[38]

Lister doesn't record what happened next to the servant in question. We don't know who she gave the food to, or why, but given the 'great quantities' spoken of, it's possible the house was wasteful, and that she had taken surplus food in order to give it to friends or family in need. Whatever happened, this servant would almost certainly never find work again in the same social circle. Anne Lister would not have spared much thought for her. In the vast majority of households, servants' lives were considered unimportant.

Anne Lister's lady's maid, Margaret Macdonald, came on the recommendation of an acquaintance, Sibella Maclean. Macdonald was from Oban, and Maclean knew of her through her ties to Scotland. The relationship between Margaret Macdonald and Anne doesn't appear to have worked, however. By 1828, Anne was wondering if Macdonald might be better off working in another house. In a letter to her aunt, Anne mentions that Macdonald is 'ashamed' to tell her friends she works at Shibden Hall.[39]

Anne Lister was regarded as an oddity in Halifax social circles, and despite all her striving, she never quite reached admission to the upper strata of society. Servants were very conscious of their employers' social standing because it reflected on them, and it may be that Margaret Macdonald had ambitions for greater things. Besides this, as a lady's maid Macdonald would have become very close to her mistress. She almost certainly became aware of Lister's sexual relations, and also of her frequent attempts to cure herself of a sexually transmitted disease via various pills and powders and washes. We can't know what Macdonald thought of Lister and her sex life, but if she felt 'ashamed' it's also possible she was shocked.

Lister's previous lady's maid, Elizabeth Wilkes Cordingley, appears to have had a closer relationship with her and to have been a favourite. When Lister's lover, Maria Barlow, asks her whether her family knew about her sexual orientation, she replies that her family and friends are 'all in a mist about it', but that her maid Cordingley knows, 'I have my own particular ways'.[40]

Lower down the servants' hierarchy there would not have been the need for such a level of trust or intimacy. Lister's requirements for a housemaid were simple: 'I want a quick steady clever person, good instruction for a good place, but who would learn any thing and clean a pigsty if I asked her.'[41]

Rural women were thought to make better servants than town girls. Anne Lister would certainly never have contemplated employing a servant from Halifax's workhouse. She would have considered such a girl far too uncouth. Harriet Baxter, a lower maid hired by Lister, was from near Stockton-on-Tees. Bridget Whitehead, a housemaid, came from Hopton, near Mirfield. Lister writes how Bridget's father, 'a respectable-looking farmer, brought her on horseback behind him'.[42] We can just imagine how anxious Bridget must have felt at being left alone at gloomy Shibden Hall, watching her father ride away.

Almost a hundred years later, Mary Schroeder noted the homesickness of her own family's maid, Cissie, who had come to the family in Halifax from Stockton-on-Tees. Cissie was,

> scarcely more than a girl, for she came from a poor family with many mouths to feed and was sent into service at an early age… In the imagination of Cissie, [our] walls were hung with portraits of the relatives she had left behind … for whenever our parents went out and Cissie was left in charge to give us our tea, she would direct the teapot with a great swish, first at one portrait and then at another. 'Here's to my father!' she would cry. Swish,

swish. 'And here's to my mother!'[43]

Young rural girls, often extremely naïve, were often sent away alone to live and work in houses far from their families. Although Cissie found work with a family she grew to love, servants could easily become prey to abusers, as seen in the previous section and the case of Rita Humphreys.

For housemaids and for most domestic servants, work was a drudgery. Eveline Askwith recalls working at a house in Luddenden at the turn of the twentieth century:

Servant at Shibden Hall 1860s (WYAS Calderdale SH-2-M-19-1-52)

> Of course all the housework was done the hard way, carpets hand-swept, and a great array of fireside brasses to be cleaned, besides lots and lots of silver. The drawing room had a lovely Adam fireplace, and how well I remember the arduous job I had cleaning the steel fireirons and big matching fender.[44]

In the early nineteenth century, housemaids like Bridget at Shibden Hall would have had nothing in the way of entertainment in their few free hours, apart from the church. For Eveline Askwith in the twentieth century, things had improved a little, but she, too, worked in a remote location, and the nearest tram was three miles away:

> Our outings were a half day a week, and on alternate Sundays we had a morning out one week, and an evening out the next, when we were supposed to attend church.

> We always went on our morning off to the village church
> … there was nowhere else to go.[45]

Askwith also wasn't allowed visitors in the house, and as for socialising with the other maids and the cook, they were never given the same free time, and so they were never all out together. This was the rule in all her situations.

The lack of time and opportunity for the servants to get together outside work must have made it almost impossible for them to unite for better working conditions. Young girls found it especially hard to insist on a fair wage. Martha Crossley, who married John Crossley in 1801, began working for a family in Warley at the age of 13. She later wrote:

> When I first went to Stock Lane I had 1/3 a week for two years. When Miss Sally died my wages were raised to 1/6 a week and there was no advance until I had been nine years and then my mother came and said if I had not £6.6s.0d a year she would take me away, and it was with difficulty that my mistress was induced to give me so much.[46]

If a servant did object to her conditions, in times of economic downturn, others were easily found to replace her, as Eveline Askwith recalled more than a century later, when in 1916 she moved on to a new employer in Sowerby Bridge: 'My starting wage of £26 a year … was the prevailing amount paid at the time, and of course servants were plentiful in those days, as alternative work was hard to come by.'[47]

Conditions for servants could often be horrendous. In the 1920s, Rita Humphreys' mother went to work as a housekeeper in London. Families in the capital were more affluent than in Yorkshire and so wages for servants were often higher, but Humphreys' mother discovered, 'her family were mean and did not intend spending their money on wages for domestics who were not willing to work every hour God sent.'[48]

Back she came to Yorkshire to work for a clergyman who made both their lives miserable by eavesdropping on their conversations and through his penny-pinching ways:

> The maid, mother and I frequently had to huddle around the gas stove which mother had deliberately lit to keep us warm. We slept in the attic where there was no lighting. We were only allowed a candle to see by... Every crumb had to be accounted for.[49]

Humphreys' mother developed phlebitis and was told by the doctor she must remain in bed for three months. Her employer was under no obligation to support or house her during her sickness, and so she lost both job and home. 'This was shattering news indeed. Where could a homeless woman with little or no money, and an illegitimate child, find a place to live for three months?'

Eventually Humphreys' mother threw herself on the mercy of a family whose rooms they had rented on holiday in happier times. Every room was let, but the family had a shed in which they'd been breeding Alsatians. Her mother had no alternative but to take it:

> These were not the days of the welfare state that we know now. But a start had been made and my mother now found herself 'on the Panel'. Through this scheme, devised by Lloyd George, my mother would receive benefits amounting to twelve shillings and sixpence per week.[50]

Rita and her mother were forced to rely on charity to eke out their benefits. The doctor's wife brought eggs, and her friends also came round with jars of jam and goodies. The Christian Scientists provided a hot meal once a week. Eventually they were rescued from their home, which was literally fit only for dogs, by Rita's great-aunt, who lived in Coronation Road, Halifax, with her family. The two families crowded together in a small, two-bedroomed terraced house.

Although some female servants in Halifax became part of the family, for the vast majority the divide between mistress and servant was strict, and for many women the work was isolating. It is probable that most working-class women in Halifax preferred to work in the mills rather than in domestic service. Of the maids and female servants listed in the 1911 census, only a small proportion were actually born in Halifax, and the rest came from outside. This may be because, like Anne Lister, employers preferred to recruit servants from rural locations, regarding Halifax working women as coarse. It maybe because women in Halifax actually preferred the independence of working in the mills to domestic service, which many of them regarded as 'skivvying'. Mill women may have felt part of a community, where they were free to marry and have children as well as work, and where they felt a greater sense of support if they should fall on hard times.

Women at Work in the Mills, Factories and Engineering

> The first object that particularly struck our attention was a group of women at Elland, loaded like asses, with bags of wool, almost fit to sink under their burdens, and countenances indicative of no good fare at home.[51]

This description comes from a letter written by George Crabtree to Richard Oastler in 1833. Crabtree goes on to note, with some irony, how little these workers fulfil middle-class expectations for women. Women in polite society should be 'alive to every tender feeling', showing 'soft compassion's sweetest tone'. Here are two very different views of women in Crabtree's time: the working classes kept in place almost like animals, and the richer women expected to be soft and feminine at all times. Both expectations confined women in their different ways.

Work for women in the textile industry in the early nineteenth century was certainly back-breaking, and in the mills it was often dangerous. Domestic service was seen by the middle classes as a more respectable form of employment for women than mill work. Many held that women servants in a middle-class household could be kept under supervision and under an 'improving' influence. However, it's likely many working-class women didn't see things this way. Domestic servants were often isolated and vulnerable, and they could be in dire straits if forced to leave employment without a reference. A disproportionately high number of prostitutes in the nineteenth century had previously been servants.[52] They were also vulnerable to abuse in the house where they were employed – the very homes that were supposed to offer a middle-class, respectable influence. Servants' chores could be even more gruelling than work in a factory, and the servants' time was not their own. Factory work offered some independence for women and allowed them to remain with their families. However, the question of mill women's morals continued to dog the nineteenth-century middle classes, and as has been seen, their 'morality' was even made a section of study in the 1892 Royal Commission on Labour.

During the decade preceding the passing of the Factory Act in 1847, there was much discussion about working conditions for women, both in parliament and in the press. Many observers of the time seemed to find the economic independence of mill women an affront.

An article in *The Spectator* in 1844 stated,

> The females themselves, says the manifesto of the Millowners, 'prefer mills to most other occupations, and even to domestic service'… There the ready comment would be, 'Who would receive as a domestic servant a girl bred in the mills?' It may be that … the slatternly love of finery, the bold unwomanly dispositions acquired by these poor creatures in the mill may render them averse to the restraints imposed by a well-regulated household. It is these unfortunate creatures who … keep up the

number of child-neglecting mothers ... and whose luckless children are left to grow up to share in turn their mothers' fate.[53]

It is interesting that besides the usual epithets thrown at mill women of the time –'unwomanly', 'child-neglecting', and so on – in this article their supposed 'love of finery' is described as 'slatternly'. This is in stark contrast to press reports about society events, where middle- and upper-class women wearing expensive dresses and jewellery are admired as 'feminine'.

Many observers who had actually visited the mills noted that far from being 'slatternly', women workers in Halifax took a great deal of care over their appearance and that of their households.

In 1850, the journalist Angus Reach visited Holdsworth's Mills at Shaw Lodge. He noted how,

Women winding yarn from creel to warp beam at Radcliffes, c.1950 (Jack Uttley Collection)

the vast majority of weavers were young women. In neatness and propriety of dress they rivalled the silk spinners [in Macclesfield] and their shawls and bonnets were hung along the walls... The girls looked hale and hearty, and Mr Holdsworth was energetic in calling my attention to their plumpness, a quality which in a large majority of cases they certainly possessed to a very fair degree... A sort of small cookshop is established near the furnace of one of the steam engines, and thither every girl who pleases brings her dinner, ready cooked ... to be readily warmed up again... Nearly 300 of these messes ... were handed out through a sort of buttery-hatch to each applicant as she shouted the number of her carding-machine, her spinning-frame, or her loom. The dinners consisted almost invariably of a portion of baked meat with potatoes, and in a few instances mushrooms. A great number had coffee and tea in little tin flagons. Altogether the dinners seemed substantial

Women machinists at Croft Myl, Halifax (Courtesy of Steve Gee)

and nourishing. I was gratified by the appearance both of the consumers and the fare consumed.[54]

Reach's letter goes on to reveal the inequality in both position and wages that was typical of women's employment in the mills and in every arena throughout this period and beyond: 'In the carding, drawing, and spinning departments, the mechanism was almost exclusively looked after by women and girls, at the low wages of 5s. and 5s. 6d. The men employed were overlookers, and earned from 15s. to 22s.'

After visiting Holdsworth's, Reach went on to Akroyd's mill on Old Lane, where he found,

> The adult males, not including the weavers, might have about 17s. a week. Female adults might average in the spinning and drawing rooms, about 6s. or 6s. 3d ... In the weaving department my informant thought that the average rate earned by men and women might be somewhat above 8s. per week.

Here, the men and women weavers appear to have been paid the same, but there was strong resistance to paying an equal wage in almost all quarters that lasted well into the twentieth century.

In 1922, at a meeting of the British Association for the Advancement of Science in Hull, Professor Francis Edgeworth, a leading expert in economics, gave his opinion that,

> Equal pay for men and women engaged on the same work is not only absurd, but unfair to men... Only a small fraction of women workers turn their wages to the same account men do. The vast majority of men have dependents to maintain, but not more than twelve percent of women workers contribute to the maintenance of anyone but themselves.[55]

It would be interesting to know where Professor Edgeworth got his figures from. At this time it was customary for women to leave work on getting married, which would mean they weren't earning a wage. Many mill women, however, carried on working after marriage because their wages were needed in the household. It was consistently thought that women's wages were not strictly necessary and their earnings were just a 'top-up' to the man of the household's wage. This view of women's work as secondary contributed to the depression in their pay, and to their continuing economic dependence on men.

It's interesting also to note how factory work was divided by gender, with some jobs being seen as men's work and some as women's. This gender division varied from mill to mill, and also varied over time.

In 1903, at the centenary celebrations for John Crossley & Sons, William Brear recalled that forty years before, 'All the young men of the villages around Halifax were seized with the ambition to become weavers at Dean Clough... The young women were fired with the same ambition; and if they could only get the employment of a setter for Crossley's, their reputation was made.'[56]

Women mending, Crossley's Carpets 1950s (Courtesy of John Saville)

Woman weaving at the Crompton loom, Crossleys Carpets 1950s (Courtesy of John Saville)

The female 'setters' prepared carpets for weaving by placing bobbins into the spindles according to a pattern. In the 1870s, Crossley's began employing women to run certain new carpet looms. Where men and women worked the same machines at Crossley's, they were paid the same rates. In 1870, Francis Crossley wrote to his manager, Mr Musgrave: 'I object to this proposed plan of paying men one price and women another; let everything be done for a man that would be done for a woman – let him have neither more nor less price… In my opinion it is the only sound course.'[57]

However, when May Abraham reported on women's employment for the Royal Commission on Labour in 1892, she noted that women at Crossley's were being paid at a lower scale than men. Their average wage was 13s 9d per week, where the men earned on average 21s 8d. When she enquired about the difference, she was told, 'In the heavier parts of the work the women require assistance which is not the case with the men.'[58]

Where employers could substitute a male employee for a woman at a lower wage, they took the opportunity. Elsewhere in the UK the introduction of women into carpet weaving led to strikes and bitter dispute, especially in Kidderminster at the Brinton's factory. Brussels weaving, in particular, was held to be men's work. At Crossley's it was done from the enormous 'H' shed which opened in 1869. It was considered an elite operation, and in Halifax the male weavers formed their own Brussels Carpet Weavers' Association. At Crossley's, Brussels weaving continued to be a higher-paid male preserve, but at another carpet mill in Halifax the men were told they must accept the same wages as women. The men refused, went on strike over it and were sacked. They were replaced at the Brussels looms with women and boys. The price paid to the male weavers had been 35s per week. The price paid to the women was 20s.[59]

During the Second World War, women at Crossley's took over some of the carpet looms that had been previously run by men. However, anecdotal evidence has it that they were 'filtered out' from these jobs when the servicemen returned. Tapestry weaving had always been held to be women's work, however, and after the war, women at Crossley's continued to do the bulk of the weaving of designs such as Axminster.

In the textile boom of the late 1940s and early 1950s, women workers were desperately needed in the worsted and woollen mills. In 1947, several women's organisations met with the Ministry of Labour at Bradford Town Hall to discuss the

Woman weaving Axminster, Crossley's Carpets (Crossley's Carpets brochure 1926)

recruitment drive. A representative of the Ministry suggested that girls should temporarily be allowed to leave school at 14 to work in spinning departments, where there was a great shortage of labour. She suggested the girls could return later to finish their education. The women present expressed themselves 'bluntly' in their replies, with this particular suggestion meeting with 'considerable protest'. Once again, girls' education appeared to be of lesser value – there was never any suggestion of boys leaving school early to fill the gaps. At the meeting the deputy lord mayor of Bradford stated that during the war women had tipped the scales of victory and that their work in the mills was of national importance. This stirring speech was slightly marred at the end by the comment that women should return if 'they wanted to see more clothes in the shops'.[60]

The need for women to work in the mills created much debate at the time and a certain amount of tension. The divide between middle-class and working-class women was still great. The textile labour shortage had created a national crisis, but recruitment drives were being solely aimed at the working classes. A woman at one conference remarked drily, 'there is still

Women at Turners Spinners, Jumples Mill c1952 (Courtesy of Richard Holt Blackburn)

a whole reserve of women to be drawn upon if one reflects upon the numbers seen at cafés and at bridge drives.'[61]

When women's labour was needed, the argument that working mothers were neglecting their children was once more forgotten. Some women raised the objection themselves that they were reluctant to leave their children, and that nursery provision was inadequate. One astonishing reply to this was that, since housing was scarce, many young couples with children were forced to live with their parents. This meant that the grandparents were on hand if the mother went to work, and, 'the problem of the supervision of the children is not as acute as it might be'.[62]

Labour in the textile industry was needed across the board at this time, both in the traditionally male jobs and the female. The unions insisted that where a woman stepped in to do a 'man's job', she should be paid the same rate as the man. Where men had to step in to do a 'woman's job', however, they should still be paid a man's rate.

The post-war years saw a boom time, but over the years there had been many downs as well as ups in the textile industry. The fluctuations in fortune are symbolised by the gradual dismantling between 1893 and 1918 of the firm of Akroyd's – once the largest worsted manufacturer in the town. Many jobs were lost during downturns in textiles, but at the same time many other trades in Halifax flourished, continuing to offer employment to women, albeit at the low end of the pay scale. Growing spending power and greater leisure hours encouraged the growth of the confectionery industry. In 1850, Joseph Dobson and his wife, Eleanor, founded a business in Elland making wedding cakes and funeral biscuits. Eleanor was the sister of William Berry, of the Berry family who founded Terry's. The business grew and Dobson's continues to manufacture sweets and lollipops.

In 1890, John and Violet Mackintosh opened a pastry-cook's shop in King Cross Lane. It was here Violet Mackintosh devised a recipe for a sweet that was a blend of traditional English butterscotch toffee and American caramel. Her toffee was a great success, and with her husband's enormous entrepreneurial flair the business grew rapidly. Mackintosh's

Women Workers at Mackintosh's PHDA/Pennine Heritage Collection
PNH02303

went on to become the largest toffee manufacturer in the world, employing thousands of women.[63]

Other confectionery manufacturers in the town included Riley Bros – whose famous toffee rolls were developed from a recipe devised by Ella Riley – as well as Meredith and Drew in Ovenden, and John Whittaker's.

John Mackintosh died in 1920, and his son, Harold, took charge of his company. A year later, Harold Mackintosh held a meeting with his employees to explain the company's new profit-sharing system. Mackintosh also outlined the company's plans to offer life insurance to both male and female office workers, but – although hundreds of women worked on the shop-floor – only male shop-floor workers would be eligible. This decision reinforces opinion of the time (as seen previously in economist Professor Edgeworth's remarks) that even though men and women had children together, it was men who were financially responsible for

Riley's Toffee works (Original postcard)

them. The women's wages were secondary. This was despite the fact that many women at the time had been left widowed after the First World War and were now providing for their families alone. Mackintosh's were generous in their offer of maternity allowance, however, which even extended to wives of employees.[64]

The Charles Horner jewellery business began in small premises in Northgate before moving to a large factory at Mile Cross, Gibbet Street, in 1905. Horner's became famous for their silver hatpins and patented thimbles. Once factory production started, they were able to bring their silver and enamel jewellery to the mass market. At its height, Horner's employed 350 people, many of them women and – before the 1918 Education Act – young girl half-timers. As in the textile industry, supervisors (overlookers) in factories were almost always male, and employers would only advertise for male supervising staff. In April 1913, for example, an advertisement appeared in the Yorkshire Post asking for a 'Man to take charge of large Enamelling Department' at Horner's'.[65]

Women soldering at Charles Horner 1914 (Courtesy of Steve Gee)

In the photo of Charles Horner's works in 1914, two young women – barely more than girls – are standing at a central island which contains open tubs of acid. The women have attached wire to the jewellery they are working on and they are about to dunk it in acid in order to remove black marks left by soldering. They have no protective clothing.

As has been seen in the chapter on child labour, accidents in the mills and factories were common. The first factory inspectors were appointed in 1833. Mill owners and their overlookers gradually began to establish safeguards, but the process was slow. Accidents continued to be serious and too often fatal.

In 1841, George Marvel, an overlooker at Lily Lane Mill, told the factory inspector, 'Accidents will occasionally happen.' His use of the word 'occasionally' does not fit the inspector's findings, which were as follows:

Women at work at Charles Horner 1914 (Courtesy of Steve Gee)

Anne Holroyde, 11 years old, was nipped in the fingers a few days ago between the two front carrier wheels, when she was drying the wheels and looking the other way. A small tin case on the gathering side would have prevented it. Another girl, Martha Molyneux, nine years old, was injured in two fingers last Tuesday between the twist wheels of a roving frame; she was picking up wastes, and inadvertently put one hand on the revolving wheel. This could very easily have been guarded.[66]

These accidents paled into insignificance when, nine years later, on 29 November 1850, a boiler exploded at the Lily Lane mill, killing twelve employees – mostly young girls – and injuring seventeen others. The loss of so many young lives shocked the people of Halifax:

Many of the most respectable and influential gentlemen of the town attended [the inquest]... The spontaneous and general abandonment of all empty theories and crotchets – the consent of the masters even to a system

> of precautions made compulsory by government; in a word, the very earnest and manifest wish of the mill owners to enter into immediate action … is the last degree satisfactory and encouraging.[67]

The coroner heard witness accounts over several days. Samuel Firth, one of the mill's owners, and Joseph Helliwell, in charge of the boiler, were both found guilty of manslaughter.

The dust and heat, the long hours of standing, the repetitive strain, and the overwhelming noise were responsible for a gradual debilitation in the health of mill workers that failed to be recognised and dealt with properly until well into the twentieth century. The 1937 Factories Act addressed a wide range of health and safety issues, including conditions affecting the welfare of workers, such as overcrowding, washing facilities, and adequate provision of seating. Women workers continued to be treated at the same level as children, with a separate section in the Act concerning regulations for Women and Young Persons.

It is worth noting that working women's fashions were often influenced by the fashions of the leisured wealthy classes. Sometimes the clothes they wore were wholly unsuited to work in a factory. One factory inspector bemoaned the invention of the crinoline.

> The garments are sometimes so extended that the dress sweeps between the two frames between which the young persons work, and the passing of two persons between the two frames, in what is called the 'alley or gate', cannot be accomplished without great liability to injury. The fashion, however, has a deep hold at the present time.[68]

By the early twentieth century, engineering had become the second most important industry in Halifax.[69] Firms such as Butler's and Asquith's had expanded rapidly from the end of the nineteenth century. There were no women workers in any of these engineering companies until the start of the First World War.

Women at Asquith's Machine Tools (Courtesy of Steve Gee)

English engineering trade unions were strong and they insisted on their members being fully trained – that is, not just trained for one machine or one process, but with enough skills to see manufacture through from start to finish. On the outbreak of war, when engineers were called up and many women had to step into their jobs, the government got round the unions' regulations by introducing what was known as the 'dilution of labour for war work'. This meant skilled jobs could be broken down into individual processes, and thus the employees working on one sole process avoided being labelled as equal workers with the trained engineers. This 'dilution' also meant companies could pay women workers less money than the men they had replaced.

Smith, Barker and Willson were a firm of lathe-makers in Ovenden. Laura Willson, a suffragette who had been imprisoned in 1907 (as we shall see in a later chapter) was the wife of one of the owners. When war broke out, Laura Willson was appointed to superintend the women's department set up by the firm. Under her guidance, the department was a great success. Willson introduced a canteen offering cheap, substantial food for the women, many of whom were malnourished. The idea caught on and was adopted in many other factories around the country. The Department of the Ministry for Munitions enlisted Willson's help in the organisation of women's munition works in the Midlands, and in 1917 she was awarded an MBE for her contribution.

After the war, Smith, Barker and Willson continued to employ women on general machine work. This caused a controversy. The 1919 Restoration of Pre-War Practices Act had forced most women to leave their wartime jobs, particularly in engineering. Servicemen returning from the war felt entitled to walk back into their previous places of employment. Laura Willson and her husband held their ground, but on 26 January 1920, an engineer called Arthur Taylor took the company before the Halifax Local Munitions Tribunal. It was put before the tribunal at an appeal that before the war, no women were employed in the firm's engineering workshops. A number of witnesses came forward to state that no women were employed in any engineering workshops they'd ever visited before the war, including in Germany.

George Willson told the tribunal that women had in fact done repetitive work in engineering, and that the repetitive nature of the women's work in his company classified it as 'semi-skilled' and not 'skilled' – and therefore women's work, and not men's. The company lost the case and was fined £50.[70]

In June 1919, as a response to the situation so many women engineers had faced in being forced to leave their jobs, Laura Willson and six other women founded the Women's Engineering Society. In September 1926, Willson headed the fourth annual conference of women's engineers at Leeds University. The *Leeds Mercury* described the conference as a group of 'plucky women' and, just as in many of today's press reports about professional women, the reporter seemed more interested in their appearance than in what they actually had to say. Much

Women at Asquith's Machine Tools (Courtesy of Steve Gee)

was made of the fact that the women were, 'shingled [that is, with hair cut in fashionable layers], permanently waved, and extremely smartly dressed'.[71]

In Laura Willson's opening address at the conference she congratulated a woman graduate from Leeds on recently becoming a Doctor of Science in Gas Engineering, and she spoke with satisfaction of the new opportunities opening up to women. It is interesting that Willson felt obliged to add that these new opportunities did not mean the majority of women would not also become wives and mothers. It's as though she was aware that many people felt threatened by women stepping into traditionally male jobs, and she felt she had to reassure her audience.[72]

In the 1920s, Laura Willson went on to achieve much success as a house builder. She confessed to having some 'sleepless nights' when starting out on her business,[73] but she was successful in building several modern housing estates for workers in Halifax. Her houses included the latest gas and electrical appliances. Some of these estates are still there today, such as the one at Club Lane in Ovenden. Willson was the first female member of the Federation of House Builders.

Laura Willson died in 1942. She led a remarkable life and was widely respected. A report in 1917, after she received her MBE, said of her: 'Gifted as a speaker, wide in her sympathies and with the courage of her convictions, she is held in high esteem among all classes.'[74]

The Halifax Building Society: 'No Female Shall Be Admitted to Any Office Therein'

The first typewriter with a qwerty keyboard was invented by the US gun manufacturers, Remington's. It was deemed ideally suited for women to use, since women were, of course, thought to have all those skills of dexterity, nimbleness of finger, etc., that men lacked. Crucially, women typists could also be paid much less than men. This, combined with women's increasing access to better education, meant that the numbers of women working in offices grew rapidly from the beginning of the twentieth century. Nowadays clerical work, from being an entirely male preserve, is seen as a 'woman's job'.

Businesses in Halifax were not slow to start employing women clerks. In 1912, John Mackintosh employed at least twenty clerks and typists.[75] In 1914, the following article appeared in the *Halifax Courier*:

> A discussion took place at the Halifax Insurance Committee last night, with reference to the work of issuing the new medical card. They originally proposed doing the work in their own premises, and hiring typewriting machines and engaging lady typists at 15*s* per week. Moving to withdraw these proposals, Mr T. H. Jones found they could not get girl typists. They

were told that no one could get them just now in Halifax. They had engaged [male] clerks, who were writing out the tickets. Mrs Willson said she was not surprised they or anyone else could not get typists at 15s per week, especially for such casual employment. They spoke of women cheapening men's jobs, yet here they were offering such a low sum. Mr T. Riley said they went very carefully into what would be the average wage in this district, and came to the conclusion that 15s was quite equal to what others offered. Mr Riley added that 15s was more than what was often paid in Halifax. Answering questions, Mr Jones said that those now addressing the envelopes could earn 27s to 30s per week.[76]

The Mrs Willson quoted in the article was almost certainly Mrs Laura Willson, the suffragette and women's rights activist. It is easy to imagine the forthright Mrs Willson asking questions and forcing Mr Jones to admit the astonishing truth that he's paying male clerks 27s to 30s per week to write out tickets. In other words, he's paying the men twice as much as he would have paid trained women typists to type them – and let's not forget that the women typists would have been doing the job more quickly, too.

With the outbreak of war many men left to join up, and the shortage of clerks in Halifax became even more acute. The Technical School, which had opened on Francis Street in 1893, offered commercial classes for young women and girls in order to help plug the labour shortage gap. One of the Technical School's pupils became the first ever female clerk at what was to become the largest building society in the world.

The Halifax Permanent Benefit Building Society was established in 1853, after a series of meetings in the Oak Room, upstairs in the Old Cock Inn – the same room where James Akroyd and other mill masters of Halifax had met twenty years previously to discuss child labour. At the society's inception a set of rules was drawn up allowing women to become members (that is, to deposit savings and take out loans). However, regarding their employment, the original rules stated plainly, 'No female shall be admitted to any office therein'.[77]

Like so many male bastions, the Halifax was forced to change when war broke out. In May 1915, 24-year old Kathleen Wilson, their first female clerk, stepped into the building society's imposing premises on the corner of Princess Street and Crossley Street. Wilson had been educated at Halifax Secondary School and later took commercial classes at the Technical School. Her father, Arthur Wilson, already worked at the society as a cashier, and it's likely Kathleen was employed on his recommendation.

It would be fascinating to know how Kathleen Wilson felt as she stepped inside the building. Did she feel nervous, or excited at starting a new position? From the facts we can gain of her life, it seems Wilson was highly capable. This was not her first job – she had previously worked in a manufacturer's office, but according to the Halifax staff magazine, she had left the job to take up 'home duties'. With no servant, Kathleen Wilson's mother, Florence Wilson, may well have needed her daughter's help with the unending chores involved in running a household. After the outbreak of war, though, other duties called, and Wilson stepped back into the workplace.

Although Kathleen Wilson couldn't see the future then, she would remain at the Halifax for the rest of her working life. She never married, being one of the 'surplus women' left single after the First World War. Wilson saw the Halifax grow to become the largest building society in the world, but unlike the male members of staff there was no route to real promotion for her. After twenty years, she had moved up the ranks to Senior Lady Clerk, but this was as far as her working life would ever take her.

More women joined Kathleen Wilson during the course of the war. In the 1918 annual report of the society, the president, Thomas Whiteley, commented that, 'every effort will be made to carry on the work of the society efficiently with the help of the patriotic and capable female workers who have joined the staff.'[78]

His words were meant to reassure the shareholders, as though they might be concerned that women weren't actually

Miss KATHLEEN WILSON
Senior Lady Clerk, Head Office

*Kathleen Wilson Halifax Building
Society Head Office 1934 (IMG/1567
Courtesy of Lloyds Banking Group plc
Archives)*

up to the job. In fact, the male staff of the Halifax were already realising what an asset their new female employees were.

At the Officials' Annual Gathering in 1917, Vice President William Ramsden had stated:

I think some mention should be made of the lady clerks. I only wish that some of them were with us this evening. Two or three years ago no one would have imagined that so much of the work of the country could be done by the women.[79]

And the women had also much to bear at home. Mr Foster, manager of the Bradford office, gave a moving testimony to the spirit of the women left to carry on as the men departed for the front:

Perhaps you have stood in the railway station when a troop train is going out. You do not hear a sound. On the one hand are the carriages filled with grim-eyed men, and on the platform stand stern-faced women-folk. There is no cheering, but the bravery of the men as they leave is reflected in the faces of the women. I have seen this sight. There was not a tear on the platform – until the train had moved out. Then the women-folk gave way, and, nearby me, one poor woman expressed the spirit of that crowd: 'I don't care now as long as I could just ho'd out while he had gone!' and I think just as we are bound to admire the magnificent spirit of the men, we are bound to admire the corresponding spirit of the women.[80]

In 1907, women had been granted a vote in municipal elections. In 1918, towards the end of the war, women over 30 were given the vote in parliamentary elections for the first time. By this time, the country was aware of just how much women could contribute in the workplace, and how much they had been underestimated.

At the 1918 Annual General Meeting of the Halifax, Sir Francis Whitley-Thomson spoke for many when he voiced just what a revolutionary period this was for women.

Do you think the ladies are going to stay where they are? They have got the vote now – [laughter] – and I for one cannot understand why if a woman is fit to vote for a municipal candidate at 21 she is not fit to vote for a parliamentary candidate until she is 30. These ladies will not be content to be only clerks. I think we may look forward at no distant date to a lady secretary – [applause] … Why should we not see a lady secretary or a lady chairman?…Joking apart, woman has been too long a chattel, and now that she has begun to be treated equally with men, we shall see some developments in the Society and other walks of life which we can hardly anticipate.[81]

It is clear Whitley-Thomson meant what he said – that women were now ambitious and would want greater things than to remain clerks – but it's telling that his speech was punctuated by laughter, and that he felt obliged to say 'joking apart'. Women were still a very long way off seeing equality in the workplace.

In fact no women rose to become company secretary at the Halifax Permanent Benefit Building Society. In 1939, Miss M. M. Kinder was the only woman among sixteen members of staff to sit and pass an examination for the Institute of Chartered Secretaries.[82] Miss Kinder was an exception. Even

Sorting the mail, Halifax Building Society Head Office 1940s (IMG/677 Courtesy of Lloyds Banking Group plc Archives)

though she'd passed the exam, she would almost certainly have left work when she married. Single women could advance up the ladder, but only into roles in which they either supervised other female clerks or else acted as secretaries to men higher up in the company. At the Halifax, this was despite the fact that the women's worth was recognised right from the early stages. In 1927, the president, Sir Enoch Hill, finished his speech at the society's annual dinner by paying, 'high tribute to the really efficient, cheerful and competent work done by the lady members of the staff. The compliments paid to the staff generally applied in a special degree to the lady members.'[83]

At the same dinner, J. B. Hey gave the following telling speech, in which he spoke of the rapid expansion of the society, and the demands this made on the staff.

> To do the work of a business that is measured by twenty
> ledgers is no mean thing, but to cope with a business
> like ours which calls for twenty scores of ledgers is a
> stupendous proposition… The part played by the juniors
> in the office is amazing and if anyone wants to know
> what real work is and how to do it I would refer them to
> those juniors, the rising generation and the immediate
> hope of the future of the staff.

Hey bemoans the carelessness of some of the staff in the
internal examinations, saying, 'Senior candidates, with years of
experience, are "plucked" in arithmetic which the youngest girls
undertake with credit and success.'

Hey goes on to say, 'Worth in the office is recognised by
promotion.' This seems a rather empty phrase to modern ears.
The worth of the female staff was obviously recognised, and
yet they were offered so little in the way of promotion and real
responsibility.

Of course a great stumbling block in the way of women's
careers during this period was the fact that they had to leave
work when they married. It doesn't appear to have been company
policy at the Halifax for women actually to be obliged to leave,
but it was certainly expected. If a woman stayed on at work after
marrying, it was noted and there had to be a good reason for it.
Eileen Hey married a Merchant Navy officer, Alan Carling, in
1941, but despite her marriage, Mrs Carling remained at work
until 1943. This change to the normal procedure is presumably
due to her husband's long absences during the Second World
War. Eileen Carling only returned to work on the death of her
husband, in 1947.[84]

When women married, they were given gifts – a canteen of
cutlery, or a clock for the mantelpiece. Married women would
be replaced with the next single young girl, and they would
almost certainly never work in the offices again.

In the list of chief executives and staff at the Halifax Building
Society head office in 1952 (which by then was on Commercial
Street), all the chief executives are male.

Typists' room, Halifax Building Society Head Office 1940s (IMG/678 Courtesy of Lloyds Banking Group plc Archives)

Of the 217 staff members, 123 (fifty-seven per cent) are female. Of these 123 women staff, only two – Mrs Carling and Mrs Bradley – are married. Of the 123 female staff, only five (less than two per cent) have senior positions. These are: chief of female personnel, general manager's secretary, chief typist, manageress (filing dept), chief agenda typist.

Of the ninety-four male staff, twenty-four (25 per cent) have senior positions, ranging from Department Manager, through Chief Cashier, to Inspector. It is not recorded in the list whether any of these men are married.[85]

The female staff at the Halifax appear to have gone about their jobs with humour and diligence. They certainly seem to have been a breath of fresh air in the dark offices on Princess Street, and they took part in staff events with flair and enthusiasm. It would be interesting to know, as the years progressed, how these women felt about seeing younger men overtake them in the company.

Halifax Building Society Ladies' Cricket Team 1926 (IMG/696 Courtesy of Lloyds Banking Group plc Archives)

In 1893, Janet Hogarth became the Bank of England's first ever clerk. Hogarth was an Oxford graduate and a skilled linguist. She later wrote of her employment, 'The girls show a zeal and zest which no boy thinks of emulating. But the trouble comes when they grow to be middle-aged women and are still kept at work only fit for beginners. They have become mere machines.'[86]

It wasn't until after the 1950s, when it became acceptable for married women to remain at work, that more opportunities opened up for the female staff.

If the officials of the Halifax Building Society in 1918 could have lived to see the year 2018, they would have been astounded to find that one hundred years after they had chuckled at the idea of 'ladies' not being content to remain clerks, a woman held one of the most senior positions in the world of finance as managing director of the International Monetary Fund, and that the two countries that had then been at war – Britain and Germany – were both led by women.

CHAPTER FIVE

Chartism, Radical Politics, and Votes for Women

Halifax Women and Nineteenth Century Radical Politics

On Monday, 16 August 1819, a peaceful crowd of around 60,000 people, including thousands of women and children, assembled in St Peter's Fields, Manchester, in a protest against poverty and in support of democracy. The local yeomanry were sent to arrest the speakers and the hussars followed them in. Many hundreds of people, including women and children, suffered serious injuries, and eighteen people died, including four women and a child.

News of the 'Peterloo Massacre', as it became known, spread rapidly, and working people came out in solidarity across the country. Anne Lister noted how everyone in Halifax was talking of 'the sad work at Manchester', and how in Halifax there was 'a crowded meeting of these radical reformers [including] 500 women in white with red caps of liberty.'[1]

Benjamin Wilson, who was born in Skircoat Green in 1824, also told how the town went into mourning. He adds:

> The women of this town were not behind the men in their love for liberty, for I have heard my mother tell of their having regular meetings and lectures at the house of Thomas Washington, a shoemaker… They, too, went

into mourning and marched in procession, Tommy's wife carrying the cap of liberty atop a pole.[2]

Women's role in political reform and the fight for the vote for their husbands and brothers has often been overlooked. There was immense popular support in Halifax throughout the century for radical workers' movements, and as Wilson states, the women were not behind the men in agitating for reform.

At the time of the Peterloo Massacre, only wealthy male landowners could vote – that is, less than five per cent of the adult population. The Reform Act of 1832 later gave the vote to the propertied male middle classes, but this didn't make a significant difference to the number of eligible voters, especially not in an industrial town like Halifax. In the election of 1832, the population of Halifax township was over 15,000, and yet there were only 536 eligible voters.[3] Nevertheless, there was enormous interest in Halifax in the elections of that year, because for the first time the town was to be represented with its own Members of Parliament. When news of the Reform Act was received in Halifax, 'one of the largest bonfires ever seen was lighted, and the town was crammed with people.'[4]

Although not eligible to vote, young Benjamin Wilson swelled the ranks of onlookers in the town on election day. He recalled standing outside the Union Cross Inn, and how, 'a procession of women came in at the bottom of the street, as though they had come from Woolshops.'[5]

No women were eligible to vote in this election, of course, but a property-owning woman such as Anne Lister was able to exercise an influence on her tenants. Ballots were public, and it was known how each man had cast his vote. Lister used her power over her tenants to persuade them to vote for her favoured Tory candidate. The Shibden estates were large, and she reckoned on being able to influence fifty voters, or almost ten per cent of the eligible electorate.[6]

It is interesting to note that in 1819, Anne Lister had written in her diary:

> This morning's post brought me the *Manchester Observer* … one of the most inflammatory radical papers published… Read a little of it aloud after breakfast … 'Reform in Parliament' is a most seditious, rousing article occupying near 2¼ columns … 'Rights of Women' is a curious list of authorities in support of the rights of women to take part in these reform meetings – to vote for representatives in the House of Commons &, in short, to be in every sense of the word, members of the body politic. What will not these demagogues advance, careless what absurdity or ruin they commit![7]

Twelve years later, Lister had inherited Shibden Hall and was herself a property owner. By this time she had stopped thinking of political rights for women as 'absurdity and ruin' and had begun to understand just how severely limited her influence was as a female.

In February 1831 she wrote: 'Why should [political rights] be withheld from any person of sufficient property and education to be fairly presumed to know how to make good use of them?'[8]

Lister was a Conservative. She drew the line at allowing people without property the right to vote, but for most people in Halifax the 1832 Reform Act, while a step in the right direction, did not go nearly far enough.

On 8 May 1838, six MPs and six working men together drew up the People's Charter. The Chartists were asking for the universal right to vote – that is, the right for all men over the age of 21. Women were not included in the term 'universal'. Despite this, thousands of women threw themselves behind the Chartist cause.

Benjamin Wilson of Skircoat Green remembered his aunt being 'a famous politician, a Chartist, and a great admirer of Fergus O'Connor [the Chartist and founder of the radical newspaper, *The Northern Star*].'[9]

These radical politics were directly related to the economic conditions of the time – conditions under which women suffered just as much and often more than men. Women were more likely than men to need to claim poor relief, for example, especially in widowhood.

In February 1838, three months before the drawing up of the People's Charter, a meeting of women, chaired by Susan Fearnley, was held in 'a large room' in Elland. The women were protesting against the Poor Laws, which deliberately made conditions in workhouses harsh in order to discourage the poor from seeking relief. Mrs Grassby, in a speech 'that made tears flow so that there was scarcely a dry cheek in the audience', proposed sending a letter of protest to the queen. Elizabeth Hanson, another powerful speaker, seconded the proposal in a way that, 'melted the hearts [of those present] and drew forth floods of tears'.

The women's letter to the queen expressed their feelings in the strongest terms:

> We, the females of Elland ... approach Your Majesty with confidence, as wives and mothers, to lay before Your Majesty our grievances; for the more we contemplate the working of the New Poor Law Amendment Act, the more deeply we are confirmed it is the most unconstitutional, unchristian, unjust, and cruel enactment that ever stained the statute book of a country calling itself free... It is unchristian, because it empowers the commissioners to break the commandment, 'That whom God hath joined together, let no man put asunder', which they have done by separating husband from wife... It is illegal, by making misfortune and poverty a crime... And it is monstrously unjust to our daughters, particularly in the bastardy clauses; for it will of necessity drive them to commit suicide and child murder, which has already gone to an alarming extent.[10]

In March 1838, Hanson and Grassby formed the Elland Female Radical Association, with the resolution that:

> Females in all ages have been the best advocates for Liberty; for we give the first impulse in forming the infant mind; therefore we deem it our duty, both as wives

and mothers, to form a Female Association, in order to give and receive instruction in political knowledge.

The women added that their aim was also, 'to co-operate with our husbands and sons in the great work of regeneration'.[11]

Many Female Associations were formed in support of Chartism throughout the country. Their struggle was not for votes for women. As historian Dorothy Thompson observes:

> Two things mark the difference between the Chartist women and the originators for the movement for the emancipation of women, which was to begin soon afterwards... Although many Chartists believed in the vote for women, it was never part of the programme of the movement... There is no suggestion that [the women] saw themselves as oppressed... They are not concerned with the right to work – they are in the main more concerned with the right to stay at home and look after their families.[12]

Abram Hanson, the husband of one of the founders of the Elland Female Radical Association, acknowledged the women's importance in the Chartist struggle, saying they made, 'the best politicians, the best revolutionists, and the best political economists... Should the men fail in their allegiance, the women of Elland, who had sworn not to breed slaves, had registered a vow to do the work of men and women.'[13]

The 1830s and early 1840s were a time of terrible hardship. We have already seen in the chapter on the card-making industry how thousands of women and children in the Calder Valley lost their work as card-setters in this period, due to the invention of a new card-clothing machine.

On 4 May 1842, the Chartists presented a petition to Parliament which had been signed by more than three million people. As well as the demand for 'universal' suffrage, they were also protesting against the Poor Laws and factory conditions. The petition was rejected.

In Lancashire, where thousands of people were out of work and 'in a wretched condition'[14], a series of protests began, including a thousands-strong march of striking workers through Manchester. In a letter to the *Manchester Guardian*, Daniel Maude, a magistrate, described the marchers as, 'led by a large party of women very decently dressed ... and nothing could be apparently more respectful and peaceable than their demeanour.'[15]

In the mills around Manchester, though, protesters were no longer prepared to remain peaceful. In a protest against their low wages, striking mill workers began to stop production in the cotton mills by removing the boiler plug from the factory steam engine.

Soon rumours began to fly that the Lancashire strikers – or plug rioters – planned to cross the Pennines and enter Yorkshire to put a stop to production in the mills round Halifax. The authorities in the town brought in special constables and even troops in preparation.

The word spread, and Yorkshire mill workers came out in their thousands. On 15 August 1842, a mob of thousands marched on Halifax from Bradford. In the meantime, thousands were marching on Halifax from Lancashire, and from Todmorden and Hebden Bridge, and other towns across the north, with the aim of drawing the plugs at Akroyd's mill and other mills in the town. Women were again in the forefront:

> The streets [of Halifax] became blocked, and it was said there were 25,000 women and men there. They were poorly clad, and many were without shoes and stockings, barefooted. The disorder became so violent that the Riot Act was read, special constables sworn in, and the military called out. The women took up positions facing the police and the soldiers, and dared them to kill them. Many people were trampled under the horses' feet, and many people were injured.[16]

An account in the *Bradford Observer* also attests to the women's prominence in the march on Halifax:

An eye-witness has told us that while the magistrates [in Halifax] at one time were reading the Riot Act, a large crowd of these Lancashire women being immediately in front of him and the soldiers, declared that they had no homes, that they might kill them if they chose, and then struck up a hymn. The music struck did not save them. Our informant says that so soon as the Riot Act had been read, the constables commenced beating the women with their staves.[17]

Frank Peel, an eyewitness to the march on Halifax, recalled:

The thousands of female turn-outs were looked upon with some commiseration by the well-disposed inhabitants, as many were poorly clad and not a few were marching barefoot. When the Riot Act was read, and the insurgents were ordered to return to their homes, a large crowd of these women, who stood in front of the

CHARTISTS' RIOTS.

Chartists' Riots (Engraving from Cornelius Brown True Stories of the Reign of Queen Victoria 1886)

> magistrates and the military, loudly declared they had
> no homes, and dared them to kill them if they liked.[18]

Several marchers were taken prisoner that day:

> At two o'clock in the afternoon, a meeting of ten to
> fifteen thousand people was held on Skircoat Moor,
> when resolutions were passed touching the 'people's
> rights', and a deputation despatched to the Mayor
> to demand the release of the prisoners that had been
> captured by the authorities during the day's 'melees'.
> The women were very excited and were heard urging
> the men to attack the prisons in which the rioters
> were confined.[19]

The authorities in Halifax decided it would be better to move
those arrested away from the town, and to take them to Elland
railway station and then by train to the prison at Wakefield. The
prisoners were to be conveyed to Elland in two omnibuses, with
an escort of six police officers and eleven hussars.

The marchers got wind of the plans and many of them left
Skircoat Moor early that morning, where they had spent the
night after the riots, in order to rescue the prisoners on their
way to the station.

Eyewitness Francis Grundy, an engineer on the railway, had
an office at Salterhebble Hill:

> My office was at the foot of the hill, just opposite
> where the road began to wind upwards from the river
> and canal. It had been built before the road was made,
> and the ground floor was below the level of the path
> … I wondered much as I entered the building at the
> multitude of persons collected in the neighbourhood,
> talking eagerly, but all busy – women as well as men – in
> rushing along the various lanes over my head with arms
> and aprons full of stones, taken from the macadamized
> heaps of blue metal placed along the turnpike road.[20]

Grundy recalled seeing the two omnibuses containing the prisoners, 'come rattling down from Halifax at a gallop, surrounded by a guard of lancers … with all the pride and pomp of a crack regiment. Bravo! They have stolen a march upon the ambush.'

The authorities had sent the prisoners away an hour earlier than planned, in order to foil the rioters. But after seeing the prisoners onto the train at Elland, the soldiers and policemen would have to come back to Halifax, and so the mob continued to collect stones in readiness to attack them on their return. When a private omnibus passed through, carrying passengers who had got off the Leeds train, the crowd assumed it was one of the prisoners' omnibuses returning full of officials. They seized the horses' heads, forcing the driver to stop. One eyewitness later recalled:

> Women, armed with tremendous bludgeons, were more violent even than the men, and the omnibus and its passengers were threatened with instant destruction. A parley, however, was held, and it having been shown to the mob that this omnibus had had nothing to do with the prisoners, a safe convoy through was guaranteed, one of the women declaring, 'it was not the passengers they wanted, it was the magistrates and soldiers, and them they would have.'[21]

Just as the private party attempted to set off, the two omnibuses and their escort also appeared, and the mob – thousands of men and women stationed in the road and the overhanging cliffs, and standing on rooftops – immediately began launching their attack of stones in earnest. The innocent passers-by were caught up in the volley of rocks and boulders. Several people were injured, including two soldiers who fell from their horses and were severely beaten.

The hussars were forced to retreat until they were joined by more troops from Halifax, and the mob could be dispersed:

> It would be impossible to describe the state of the town
> at this period. The bitter imprecations of the rioters – the
> muttered curses, not loud, but deep, uttered against the
> soldiers – the shrieks of women, the blank and blenched
> countenances of the townsfolk… It was a sight very
> foreign to the industrious character and commercial
> habits of the quiet and orderly town of Halifax.[22]

These were momentous events, and as eyewitnesses reported,
women were in the thick of them.

Although tens of thousands of marchers had converged
on Halifax, within a very short time peace was restored to the
'quiet and orderly town'. The plug riots of 1842 quietly and
swiftly died away, but the Chartists' fight for the vote for all men
continued.

In 1847, five years after the riots, Ernest Jones stood as a
Chartist parliamentary candidate for Halifax. Jones was the
people's choice, and had all people been eligible to vote, he would
probably have been elected with a landslide victory. Jones failed
to be elected, but won eighteen per cent of the votes, which in
the circumstances was an astonishing achievement.

After the election, the women of Halifax arranged an
enormous tea party for Jones at the Oddfellows' Hall. With
guests numbering around 1,300, planning for such an event
must have been a tremendous feat in itself. Besides feeding the
vast crowd with 'the choicest viands in the greatest profusion',
the women arranged for an orchestra and for decorating the
hall with paintings, banners, laurels, and 'a profusion of choice
flowers throughout'.[23] The event was an enormous success.
Benjamin Wilson later recalled:

> I was at the first sitting down, which was largely composed
> of women. Some had their caps beautifully decorated
> with green ribbons, others had green handkerchiefs, and
> some even had green dresses. I have been to many a tea
> party in my time, but never saw one to equal this.[24]

Ernest Jones was arrested the following year, on the flimsiest of evidence, for holding a public meeting. At his trial he claimed people had learned that petitioning was no longer of any use, and the Chartists now wished 'to demonstrate the public opinion by more apparent means'.[25]

The Chartists had previously delivered a petition signed by more than three million to Parliament, but their wishes had been ignored. Jones's words would echo the thoughts of the suffragettes fifty years later, when petitions on behalf of women met with similar dismissal.

The 1867 Reform Act, twenty-five years after the plug riots, finally gave the vote to every male adult householder living in a borough constituency, and to male lodgers paying more than £10 rent. Voting numbers across the country were doubled, and more than quadrupled in Halifax.

No longer content to be preparing tea parties for the men, also in 1867 a group of women in Manchester formed the National Society of Women's Suffrage. The women of Halifax were not far behind those across the Pennines, and a Halifax branch of the society was formed in the 1870s.[26]

And so began the long struggle for votes for women.

The Halifax Suffragettes

On 12 February 1873, the Halifax branch of the National Society of Women's Suffrage held a meeting at the Mechanics' Institute in Halifax (now the YMCA). One of the key speakers was Lydia Becker, founder of the society, who had travelled from Manchester. Support for the women's movement was growing, and it wasn't long before politicians were tapping in. The year after this meeting, Lord Frederick Cavendish, Liberal MP, enlisted Lydia Becker's support at a Liberal meeting in Todmorden. Standing with him on the platform, Becker expressed confidence in his Lordship, the Liberal Party and Gladstone's government.[27] Becker – and thousands of other women – were to be cruelly let down. Just a few months later, back at the Mechanics' Institute in Halifax, Cavendish declared he would not support the extension of the franchise to women, because his wife did not want it.[28]

Over the next eight years, the women of Halifax held repeated meetings in the town on the subject of the vote. Between 1867 and 1884, women's suffrage was debated in Parliament every year but one. The women were to suffer an enormous disappointment when the 1884 Reform Act enfranchised millions of working-class men, but no women. In the twenty years after this Act, there were only three parliamentary debates on the subject of female suffrage.[29]

At the turn of the twentieth century, women in Britain were still no nearer having the vote. There were also no female jurors or Justices of the Peace, no female solicitors or barristers, no female employees of the Halifax Building Society, no women in either the House of Commons or the House of Lords, no women allowed to become full members of either Oxford or Cambridge University, no women in numerous professions, from stockbroking to veterinary science.

Just as the Chartists had done over half a century previously, campaigners for women's suffrage petitioned Parliament repeatedly. A petition signed by over a quarter of a million women had been presented in 1896. In 1901, a petition signed by over 29,000 Lancashire textile mill workers. In 1902, a petition of more than 33,000 Yorkshire women textile workers. Just as with the Chartists, the petitions of these women led nowhere.

The National Union of Women's Suffrage Societies, or the 'suffragists' as they came to be known, was led by Millicent Fawcett and formed in 1897. The Halifax Women's Suffrage Society immediately became affiliated to it. The suffragists were prepared to continue with these tactics of civil persuasion and lobbying ... but the mood was changing.

In 1903, Emmeline Pankhurst founded the Women's Social and Political Union at her home in Manchester. The fight for the vote was about to take a dramatic turn. As Mrs Pankhurst later wrote: 'Deeds, not words, were to be our permanent motto.'[30]

Emmeline Pankhurst was an astute woman, a charismatic leader, and a canny politician. She set up the WSPU to fight

Meeting of the WSPU leaders 1906-7 Flora Drummond, Christabel Pankhurst, Annie Kenny, Emmeline Pankhurst, Charlotte Despard with two others (LSE library 7JCC/O/02/109)

for the vote on the same terms as the men – that is to fight for votes for women of property. However, Pankhurst knew that the voice of the WSPU would be much louder with the backing of the working classes – especially the working women of the textile industry in Lancashire and Yorkshire. The time was right, too, for more working women to join the struggle. Working-class women were now far better educated than they were during the Chartist uprising of 1842, and they had more time at their disposal. Although they still worked long hours, they weren't the cripplingly long hours they'd worked before the Ten Hour Act was introduced.

The Pankhursts paid regular visits over the Pennines to drum up support. In August 1905, Emmeline Pankhurst spoke for an hour at a meeting of members of Todmorden Trades Council. She told them that Winston Churchill, whom she referred to as, 'a rising star of the Liberal Party', had stated he would not support the Women's Enfranchisement Bill as it only offered the vote to wealthy women. Pankhurst had then asked him why the government didn't introduce universal adult suffrage. Churchill's reply was, 'he could not do that because it would enfranchise the whole of the women, and we could not do with the country being governed by women'.[31]

Faced with this type of intransigence, it's little wonder women were beginning to consider more radical methods to get their voices heard.

The Independent Labour Party had strong support in Halifax at the turn of the twentieth century. In autumn 1905, Christabel Pankhurst came to speak at the Halifax branch of the ILP in their premises on St James's Street.[32] Halifax women Laura Willson and Mary Taylor were both involved in the ILP, and Laura Willson chaired the meeting.

Laura Willson and Mary Taylor, along with Dinah Connelly and young Lavena Saltonstall, who had moved to Halifax from Hebden Bridge, were great friends. In 1906, they became key members of the Halifax branch of the new Women's Labour League.[33] Its founder, Margaret MacDonald, wife of Ramsay MacDonald, looked on the Women's Labour League as a channel to persuade more women into the Labour movement. For some, though, the formation of a separate Labour league for women risked cutting them off from the actual work of the ILP. Others even spoke of it as 'teas and twaddle'.[34] However, with outspoken women such as Willson, Taylor, Connelly and Saltonstall in the thick of it, the Women's Labour League in Halifax was never going to revolve around genteel lunches. And so it proved.

On 1 July 1906, a tram went out of control coming down the steep gradient at New Bank. The driver, Thomas Chadwick, tried desperately to apply the brakes, but the tram picked up speed, shooting on to North Bridge 'like a rocket'. Here it jumped the points and overturned. Two people were killed and many injured.[35] In the steep hills around Halifax, the tramways were notoriously dangerous. The inquest recorded a verdict of accidental death, but Halifax Council dismissed Chadwick, appearing to blame him for the accident. Lavena Saltonstall, of the Women's Labour League, had a biting way with a pen. She wrote a letter to the *Halifax Guardian* defending Chadwick and blaming council penny-pinching for the accident.[36]

Where there was working men's strife, the WSPU was not slow to take advantage. Against the backdrop of the looming tram workers' strike, the Women's Labour League organised a demonstration in Savile Park to meet suffragette Annie Kenney, recently released from imprisonment for protesting outside Cabinet Minister Herbert Asquith's house. The suffragettes had grown in notoriety, and a large crowd gathered to hear what Kenney had to say. She told them, 'she often found people gathered together just to see what kind of female hooligans she and her colleagues were.' Kenney was an entertaining speaker. When faced with scornful laughter she spoke wittily and presciently of the great movements in the past which had begun with ridicule and which were now talked of seriously.[37]

The tram workers declared their intention to strike, and it was rumoured that the council were bringing in black-legs from Southport and Wakefield, and even as far away as Brighton. On 1 September 1906, thousands gathered outside the tramway depot to see how the council were going to run the trams. The crowd was mainly good tempered, but eggs and stones were thrown at the 'knobsticks' (black-legs), and there was special derision for local tram drivers who were continuing

Mary Taylor (Leeds Mercury April 16th 1907)

to work. As in the plug riots, journalists noted, 'The women were especially demonstrative.'[38]

The women of the Halifax Women's Labour League certainly played a large role in drumming up support for the strikers. The next day, a mass meeting was held in Savile Park, attended by around 15,000 people. Posters had gone up all round Halifax proclaiming that Lavena Saltonstall would be a speaker from one of the 'waggons' (carts). Saltonstall was a great letter writer, but painfully shy. At the last minute, she asked someone else to read out a letter on her behalf. She apologised in her letter, claiming she 'could not tackle an audience of two, including herself'. She went on to give a spirited attack on the 'arrogant' members of the Town Council, saying, 'Alderman Hey was too expensive a luxury for the rate-payers, and the sooner they wrote him ex-Chairman of the Tramways Committee, the better it would be.'

Reports said, 'The audience punctuated the reading of this letter by frequent rounds of applause and laughter.'[39]

On 13 September, the Women's Labour League held an open meeting in which they advocated boycotting the trams. The strikers' slogan was, 'Walk and Win'.

'One straight-limbed damsel [at the meeting] declared that she would walk until she was bow-legged.'[40] The 'straight-limbed damsel' was almost certainly Lavena Saltonstall, who during the strike walked or cycled everywhere, as did Mary Taylor.[41]

Entering the public arena meant these women needed to learn new skills and to push themselves in ways in which they were not accustomed. This took courage, especially at a time when women were expected to remain firmly at home, in their own sphere. Lavena Saltonstall continued to try and overcome her fear of public speaking. At a Women's Labour League meeting towards the end of the tram workers' dispute, she got up to give a speech but only managed to stutter out one or two words before apologising and resuming her seat. The other women at the meeting evidently sympathised with her.[42]

As the strike dragged on, and it seemed certain the men would lose, the atmosphere in Halifax grew tense. Reaction to the involvement of the Women's Labour League was mixed. The *Leeds Mercury* took a hard line against both the strikers and the women. Towards the end of the strike it ran an article headlined, 'Women's Speeches Incite Youths to Violence'.

It was claimed that after a Women's Labour League meeting in Prospect Street, where they had apparently given speeches, 'inciting youths to violence against "black-legs"', a few young men had thrown stones, smashing windows. When charged, the magistrate told the court: 'It was to be regretted that the persons who incited the lads to do this damage ... were not before them.' He added, 'There were some foolish women going about, seeking to make themselves famous, but they were only making themselves notorious.'[43]

The women's actions may have been questionable – according to the same article, they had reportedly advocated 'making things uncomfortable for those providing black-legs with lodgings'. However, none of the male ILP members (men such as James Parker, who later became Halifax's first Labour MP) were ever accused of 'seeking to make themselves famous' by speaking out in support of the strike. Reading between the lines of the magistrate's speech, one gets the impression he is censoring the women for having the temerity to attract people's attention. Their place was in the home.

In October 1906, suffragette Annie Kenney returned to Halifax to speak at a packed meeting of the Women's Labour League. She expressed her sympathy for the striking men, and, employing a political tactic that was increasingly used by the WSPU, she melded the strife with women's demand for the vote.

She told the members, 'Women must get their political freedom, so that at the next election they will be able to express their opinions through the vote.'[44]

The tram workers' strike ended in failure, leaving many of the striking men out of work. The council had simply filled their jobs with black-legs. After the failure of the strike, many of the women involved in the Halifax Women's Labour League were filled with an even greater desire to fight injustice – and the biggest injustice they faced themselves was their lack of a democratic right to vote. Without it, how could they be taken seriously in politics?

At the beginning of 1907, support for the Women's Social and Political Union was swelling across the country, including in Halifax. The personalities and determination of women such as Willson, Taylor and Saltonstall drew the attention of WSPU headquarters in Manchester.

On 2 January 1907, a letter appeared in the *Yorkshire Evening Post* headlined, 'Miss Mary Gawthorpe's Call to Yorkshire Women'. Mary Gawthorpe was a leading member of the WSPU. In her letter, she appealed 'to the many thousands of women' who read the paper, saying: 'Many [Yorkshire] women have definite political sympathies. To these I would suggest that the way to make their political efforts rightly effective is to join some branch of the Women's Party which strives for the political emancipation of women.'

Suffragette march in Heptonstall 1908 (PHDA/Alice Longstaff Collection ALC02057)

Gawthorpe urged all such women to 'postcard her at once' and she would arrange visits and literature. She left her address as 9 Warrel's Mount, Bramley.

Gawthorpe must already have arranged a meeting with the Halifax women before publication of this letter, because the very next day she arrived in Halifax. Jill Liddington, in her book *Rebel Girls*, describes how Gawthorpe was met at Halifax station by Laura Willson, whose house she was to stay in. The women called a meeting at Halifax Socialist Club, and it was then that the Halifax branch of the WSPU was formed. Seventeen women enrolled, and Willson was elected secretary.[45]

Dramatic events were about to unfold. Very shortly afterwards, Emmeline Pankhurst herself caught the train to Halifax to visit, 'her friends Mrs Taylor and Mrs Willson', and to attend meetings. As her train passed through Hebden Bridge, Pankhurst overheard two men discussing the fustian weavers' strike in the town, which had been going on for six months. Pankhurst was an expert at gaining publicity. On hearing about the strike, her ears pricked up immediately, and as soon as she reached Halifax she asked the women to fill her in on the details.

The Hebden Bridge weavers' strike was a golden opportunity, and one that Pankhurst seized with speed and aplomb. It's likely that suffragette intervention in the weavers' strike had already been arranged through Hebden Bridge native Lavena Saltonstall.[46] This was a time when telegrams were the nearest thing to instant messaging, and only a handful of people had telephones. It is perhaps unlikely that the WSPU presence could have been arranged within a couple of weeks of Pankhurst's train journey, but given her extraordinary organisational ability, it is possible.

On Monday, 28 January, 400 striking weavers and a brass band filled the centre of Hebden Bridge. The demonstration itself was organised by the Hebden Bridge Trades and Labour Council, who it said had 'enlisted the help of the Women's Social and Political Union'. News that prominent suffragettes were coming to the town spread like wildfire. Crowds turned up to see them, including many who had no involvement in the strike.

The headline in the local paper later ran: 'WOMEN'S CAMPAIGN SETS THE TOWN ABLAZE WITH EXCITEMENT.'[47]

The article went on, 'The introduction of the suffragist women into Hebden Bridge last night undoubtedly aroused the town, and excitement reached fever heat.' Mrs Pankhurst was accompanied by Mrs Willson and Mrs Taylor, 'of Halifax tram strike fame'.

The Pankhursts were masters of the art of promotion. The Co-operative Hall was too small to hold the crowd, so Emmeline Pankhurst obliged by giving a rousing ad hoc speech outside, on the steps at Bridge Mill, to those who couldn't find seats. Meanwhile those inside the Co-operative hall drummed the floor with their feet, waiting with good-natured impatience for her to come in. When she finally did, taking her place on the platform with Saltonstall and Taylor, the crowd erupted in cheers. They were not disappointed. Pankhurst was a consummate speaker and knew exactly how to hold a crowd. What followed was a masterclass in political public speaking.

She began by claiming she was interested in strikes, 'as a woman', because the people who suffered most in such discord were the, 'dear little children, with no responsibility at all'.

Sympathy for the children was a guaranteed crowd-pleaser. With her trademark humour, she rallied the people by saying,

> Quiet, persuasive methods, as she knew in another campaign (laughter) were all right to a certain point, but the time came when those methods needed something more to back them up. She saw that they in Hebden Bridge wanted something of a more aggressive kind, if they wanted to bring the struggle to an end.

In the next breath, and rather contradicting herself, she told those present that countries such as Australia had brought in a system of arbitration, and she inferred that this sensible practice of talking through dispute was the result of Australian women having been given the vote. She went on to empathise with the crowd, telling them that the strikers had been badly treated, that they had a legitimate case, and that what they needed was publicity. Enlisting the help of the WSPU would certainly provide them with that. Pankhurst finished her speech by moving seamlessly into women's suffrage, promising that once women had the vote, the right people would be elected and there would be a fair wage for all.

Her speech was met with tremendous cheers. Mary Taylor got up next, and she followed in a stirring vein, telling the crowd, 'she couldn't understand why the women of Hebden Bridge were so peaceful'.[48] She went on to say that during the tram strike in Halifax, 'we had things lively, and one wonders why you have been so peaceful after the example we have set you.'[49]

It was possibly not a good idea to mention the Halifax tram strike. Despite the work of the women, and much agitation in the town, the strike had ended with failure and with the loss of many jobs.

Laura Willson, with typical common sense, finished the meeting with a resolution that the people present, 'call upon the Government to form legally appointed boards of conciliation for the settlement of trades disputes'. Copies of the resolution were sent to the prime minister.

Tensions were already high in Hebden Bridge before the meeting. Several mill owners had begun to import workers from Luddenden and Midgley. The fustian weavers would have been well aware that the tram strike in Halifax had ended in defeat through imported workers. It was the middle of a bitterly cold and snowy winter, and the strikers' families would have been anxious about having enough coal and enough money to pay the doctor to treat the endless winter illnesses that beset their children. Non-union workers had already been mobbed as they left work at Shackleton's mill. On Heptonstall hill, stones had been thrown down at Shackleton's house, smashing windows.

It took very little more to stir the simmering anger, and the visit from the suffragettes appears to have ignited it.

Over the days that followed, the strikers continued to harass non-union weavers leaving work. Police filled the streets, and as the factory hooters blew for the end of the shifts, confrontation began. Suffragette Jennie Baines of Stockport held an open air meeting in the town. She was given a court summons for intimidation after joining the crowds hooting and jeering outside the houses of two mill owners, Shackleton and Thomas.

Three days after attending the meeting with Emmeline Pankhurst, Laura Willson was back in Hebden Bridge. Prominent suffragettes Adela Pankhurst and Mary Gawthorpe, too, came to the town. Open air meetings were held and the streets were once more thronged with striking weavers. Willson was arrested for handing out 'seditious literature'. She had been handing out leaflets to the crowd, including one entitled, 'Suffragettes and Their Unruly Ways'.

The following night, the striking weavers met again at the Co-operative Hall. Adela Pankhurst and Mary Gawthorpe spoke to the crowds, and once more they marched through the snowy streets, first up the hill to the house of William Thomas, where they jeered and hooted and sang mocking songs, and then back up the other side of the valley to Heptonstall Road and Roger Shackleton's house. The inflamed crowd must have made an intimidating sight. Forewarned, the police had surrounded Shackleton's house, but the crowd was large. The suffragettes appealed for hooting, and stones were thrown and windows smashed.

A few days later, Laura Willson appeared at Todmorden court with Jennie Baines. Both were sentenced to a forty shilling fine or fourteen days' imprisonment. Willson stated that she objected to the constitution of the court because it consisted of men only, and she refused to plead unless she could be professionally represented by a female lawyer. After refusing to pay the fine, both women were sent to Armley Gaol in Leeds.

Laura Willson was the first Yorkshire suffragette to be imprisoned in a Yorkshire gaol. Her time in prison proved a turning point for her. The previous year, Willson had been working for the cause of the Independent Labour Party. Now her prime objective became the fight for the vote.

During the riots in Hebden Bridge, she had claimed she would, 'show the men of Hebden Bridge how to go to prison... Going to prison was not such a horrible thing, after all. There was a going to prison that was glorious, and this will be an instance.'[50]

In fact, although she spoke bravely and wittily about prison when she was released, the reality of spending fourteen days at Armley appears to have been a terrible experience. Besides the conditions in this grim gaol, Willson also had to leave her 5-year-old son in the care of her husband, which must have been a terrible wrench. When Willson's husband visited, they were forced to talk to one another through iron grilles, in between which was a yard long gap where the warder sat, listening to every word. Willson wore a coarse blue prison uniform. Without proper washing facilities, she later said she looked 'a scarecrow'. Despite her humour, it must have been a humiliating experience. Willson later said she regretted asking her husband to visit her, as he was distressed on her behalf. Added to this there was the winter chill of the cells, the no doubt unclean clothes and bedding, the humiliation of the constant observation and lack of privacy, besides the inedible food. Willson afterwards said brightly, 'the tea was horrid, and the suet pudding would make a very good substitute for leather, if the cobbler was hard up'.[51]

It was a sobering experience, but Willson was tough, and far from cowing her, her time in prison only strengthened her resolve to carry on fighting. She declared, 'she was glad women from Halifax and other parts of the country have been arrested, for it shows the movement is not confined to a few, but is general.' She also declared jokingly that in prison, 'she was better treated than the majority of women in Halifax, and she had less work to do.' She added, 'Instead of killing our spirits, they have only made it stronger.'[52]

A contingent of women from Halifax caught the 6 a.m. train in order meet Willson on her release. She told waiting journalists, 'I went to gaol a rebel, but I have come out a regular terror.'[53]

The Hebden Bridge Labour and Trades Council and members of the Manchester WSPU organised another meeting at the Co-operative Hall to welcome Willson home. Halifax women Dinah Connelly and Lavena Saltonstall were also at the meeting, and Willson was given an enthusiastic reception. It was here that she confessed that, 'she had often sat in prison and cried', but added that she had, 'come out more determined than ever to do something'.[54] The authorities made a mistake in imprisoning a woman like Willson. Far from being a deterrent, it only strengthened her resolve to continue to fight for the vote.

Emmeline Pankhurst had offered the striking weavers in Hebden Bridge publicity through the involvement of the suffragettes. Unlike the middle-class Pankhursts, Laura Willson must have understood very well the realities of life for these weavers. She had been a weaver herself, and had worked as a part-timer from the age of 10. And yet Willson appears to make no mention of the weavers' strike in her interviews and speeches on leaving prison. At least, all that is reported in the press is her determination to fight for women's suffrage. It must have been a blow to the striking weavers to find there was no mention of their struggle in the local papers on Willson's release.

Leslie Goldthorpe was president of the Hebden Bridge Local History Society in the 1950s, at a time when there would have been residents of the town still living who were eyewitnesses to the events surrounding the strike. In an essay, Goldthorpe wrote:

> I have exploited the memories of elderly people among us whose families were involved directly or indirectly in the fustian weavers' strike … Many people in the district considered that the intervention of the suffragettes was to be regretted, and only resulted in exacerbating an already embittered situation.[55]

With the surge in support for the WSPU across the north, Emmeline Pankhurst and the other leaders of the organisation now had many hundreds of working women to call on to help with the cause. While Willson was in prison, several Halifax women answered the WSPU's call to head down to London.

On 9 February, a few days before the opening of Parliament, Millicent Fawcett of the National Union of Women's Suffrage Societies (the less militant suffrage campaign group) led a procession of many thousands of women through London. The accents of hundreds of northern women were joined to those of the Londoners: 'Many were wearing clogs and shawls, and these women of the North were a unique sight to the Londoners.'[56]

In the meantime, the WSPU leaders knew full well that the king's speech at the opening of Parliament would contain no mention of votes for women. They in turn had organised a meeting at Caxton Hall for the day after his speech. From there, the women were to march on Parliament.

Arthur Taylor, an ILP member and councillor, was at Halifax station to see his wife off on her journey to London to join the WSPU march, as was Dinah Connelly's husband Charles, a mason. Both men supported their wives. Taylor later said, 'Many Halifax women are prepared to go to [WSPU] headquarters if their services are required. Only a telegram is wanted to fetch them up.'[57]

The women were aware when they travelled down to London that going to prison was a risk, but it was a risk they were prepared to take.

The WSPU march was typically well coordinated. The hundreds of women coming into London from the north were accommodated in the homes of other suffragettes. On 13 February, 700 women, organised into groups to appear from different directions and at different times, advanced on Parliament with the intention of entering the House of Commons. They were met by mounted police:

> The plans laid by the leaders were very comprehensive…
> The scene in the open space between St Margaret's Church and the House of Commons was an amazing one. The women fought a pitched battle with the police, dozens of whom were mounted. Many of the women were rather badly hurt in the melee, being half-trampled underfoot by the horses… Arrests were made

in all directions, a procession of shouting women and perspiring constables entertaining the thousands of spectators who lined the roadway.[58]

The Halifax women were in the second wave of protesters, arriving at the House in the evening. Again they were met with mounted police, who rode at them with their horses. Women were dragged or bodily carried from the doors of the House and thrown to the ground. Their attempts to enter lasted for hours. By the end of the day, fifty-four women had been arrested. One of those women was Mary Taylor of Halifax. She was charged with disorderly behaviour and held at Holloway Prison until 27 February. When she was released, along with several other suffragettes, they were met at the gates of the prison by supporters and a brass band, who accompanied them to the nearest tube station. Mary Taylor caught the train home on the day of her release. On her arrival at Halifax station she was greeted as a heroine by hundreds of supporters.

Suffragettes in Heptonstall (The Jack Uttley Collection)

By this time Laura Willson, too, had been released from Armley, and she will have been at Halifax station to greet her friend. Despite the shock of her own imprisonment, Willson declared she was sorry to miss the events in London, and that she intended to write to the 'London people' to inform them she was ready to take part whenever they needed women for 'active work'.[59] Willson was soon to be granted the opportunity.

On 3 March, Emmeline Pankhurst herself was again back in Halifax for a meeting arranged at the Theatre Royal to welcome Taylor and Willson home from their imprisonment. Pankhurst had another reason for being in the town. There was shortly to be a by-election, and the WSPU was keen to sway voters against the Liberal government which had consistently held out against giving women the vote. The meeting was packed. During the evening, Taylor and Willson were each given a framed picture of Mrs Pankhurst as a gift.[60] The gesture does seem a little egotistical – Mrs Pankhurst was to develop a reputation in some quarters as a despotic leader – but these were different times, and it's likely the two women were very pleased with their present.

Less than three weeks after this meeting, Willson would have her chance to take part in 'active work' in London. On 8 March 1907, a bill in support of women's suffrage failed to get any support in the House of Commons. The WSPU decided to answer this rejection with another march on Parliament. The northern women in their clogs and shawls had made an impression in London during the recent NUWSS demonstration, and Pankhurst knew how to stage an event. This time they were also looking for greater numbers in order to succeed in gaining entry. There was a concerted effort to persuade working women from Lancashire and Yorkshire to answer the call and travel south.

Laura Willson, Lavena Saltonstall and Dinah Connelly were among the women who took the train from Halifax to London. Once more there was a meeting at Caxton Hall, and once more the women marched on the House. By the end of that day of protest, 20 March 1907, seventy-four women had been arrested. A quarter of the women arrested were from the West Riding, and they included Willson, Saltonstall and Connelly. Lilian

Cobbe and Lizzie Berkeley of Hebden Bridge WSPU were also arrested. The women were given the choice of a fifty-shilling fine or fourteen days in Holloway prison. They all opted for prison.

At the court hearing, Willson denied resisting the police. She told the magistrate, with her usual humour and spirit, 'I wanted to go into the House of Commons, and it was the police who resisted me.'[61]

Willson faced another two weeks in prison, plus separation from her husband and young son. Coming so soon after her imprisonment in the grim conditions at Armley, this must have been hard for her indeed, but she chose imprisonment.

On 30 March, George Willson made the journey down to London to visit his wife. This was again a distressing experience for him. He thought Willson was looking ill, and he wanted to pay her fine and have her released. Willson knew the ILP conference in Derby was coming up, and so allowed herself to be persuaded.

Before joining the WSPU, none of the Halifax women had had any brush with the law. Willson later claimed the two doses of prison had played on her nerves.[62] However, her imprisonment did nothing to deter her. The Halifax suffragettes were welcomed back after their imprisonment, and the following months continued to be busy ones. Willson spoke at several meetings. In July 1907 the ILP and Pankhurst, along with Willson and many other local suffragettes, were frantically busy again, after a by-election was called in Huddersfield.

Female members of the Women's Labour League, such as Laura Willson, did a tremendous amount, both behind and in front of the scenes, for the ILP. It seemed, though, that the work done by the Women's Labour League was still not taken seriously, and it was beginning to appear to Willson that it was indeed a mistake to have a separate women's branch of the party. Earlier that year, at the Labour Party's conference in Belfast, there had been only one female speaker. This speaker had urged the party to consider the solitary paragraph in their report that concerned the formation of the Women's Labour

League, telling them, '[The Women's League] might be a very powerful weapon for good in the hands of the Labour party.'[63]

Her prediction proved true. At the Huddersfield by-election in July 1907, the Labour party won a dramatic victory in the town. Their candidate, Victor Grayson, was elected. Female canvassing and leafleting, and the meetings held in Huddersfield by Pankhurst and other suffragettes, had played a significant role in the Labour party victory.

Laura Willson was becoming increasingly frustrated at having no formal voice in party politics, and her patience was running out. In 1908, she spoke at the Women's Labour League conference in Hull: 'We as a Labour League are to be allowed to work (at our expense) in the Parliamentary elections, but we have no voice in the Parliamentary policy of the party.'[64] She also said that, 'she would personally remain outside the National Labour Party if she could not be admitted on the same terms as the men.'[65]

Late 1907 and early 1908 were times of change and readjustment in the women's campaign. In September 1907, there was a dramatic split within the WSPU. Some of its members were unsatisfied with the way the organisation was being run, and with the violent tactics increasingly being used. Emmeline Pankhurst was certainly charismatic, but she appears to have been an autocratic leader. At a meeting on 10 September, she as good as demanded loyalty to her leadership. Several women – including Charlotte Despard and Teresa Billington-Greig – left to form a new group called the Women's Freedom League. The new group continued to break the law, for example by refusing to pay taxes, but they did so via peaceful means.

This split caused consternation in towns such as Halifax, where the women were far removed from the internal politics going on in London. Class differences in Edwardian times were still as great as they'd been in the previous century. Although Pankhurst had called the Halifax women, Willson and Taylor, 'her friends', it's highly unlikely she would have invited them to the social events of her circle, unless there was a political reason to do so. The previous year Alice Milne, a working-class supporter from Manchester, had visited the WSPU offices in London and found the place to be, 'full of fashionable ladies in rustling silks and satins ... if any of our Adult Suffrage Socialist friends could have looked into that room, he would have said that more than ever ours was a movement for the middle classes and upper classes.'[66]

Right from the beginning, the aim of the WPSU had been to gain the right for women to vote on the same terms as men. At that time men had to be householders, or at least registered house occupiers, before they were eligible for the electoral roll. To struggle for votes for women on these terms meant struggling for political rights for middle-class and relatively wealthy women.

This had always put the Halifax branch of the WSPU in a strange position. If they were fighting for the vote on the WSPU's conditions, they were not therefore fighting for the vote for themselves.

In October 1907, Laura Willson and others attended the meeting organised by the new Women's Freedom League. There had been much discussion in Halifax, and the women were torn. They had already made tremendous sacrifices under the leadership of the WSPU.

Willson told the meeting that they were there to find out more about what was happening in London. She added, 'Our women are not women in politics, but they have just come along because of the women having been sent to prison.'[67]

Being imprisoned was no small thing for women like Willson, and it had had a dramatic effect on many of them. Besides their concern over the split in the WSPU, the women also faced the real danger of further confrontation and intimidation. The mood towards the militant suffragettes in Yorkshire was beginning to turn ugly.

In early December 1907, Laura Willson chaired a public meeting of the suffragettes at a packed town hall in Huddersfield. The atmosphere in some parts of the hall was decidedly unwelcoming. One newspaper reported, 'Nervous and agitated, Mrs Willson faced the prospect with a good show of bravery.'

When the heckling continued, Willson warned disrupters they would have to leave if they didn't quieten down. A woman shouted, 'You shouldn't do it to other folk, then!' Shortly afterwards, fierce fighting broke out. The police were forced to step in and several young men were thrown bodily out of the hall.[68]

A few weeks later, in January 1908, Willson travelled to Lancaster to meet Jennie Baines, the Stockport suffragette who had been imprisoned with her in Armley. Herbert Asquith was holding a meeting in the town, and special precautions had been taken to prevent suffragettes entering the venue. No women were allowed to buy tickets until the day of the event. Willson managed to infiltrate it, and when Asquith began speaking she shouted, 'But what about the women, Mr Asquith?'

According to reports, there was 'much interruption for some time' while Asquith stood with 'an impassive face.'[69]

Willson was ejected from the meeting. She went to join Baines outside on the 'lurry' from which she was addressing a peaceful gathering. When the meeting inside had finished, however, and the crowd came out, several people attempted to push the lurry over a parapet and into the gardens 6 feet below. Sympathisers managed to prevent them, but there was then a cry of, 'Rush them into the canal!'

> Detective Johnson and two constables formed a bodyguard for the two suffragists. Mrs Baines and her husband got off on the far side of the lurry, and managed to escape, but hands were laid on Mrs Wilson [*sic*] and her clothing ripped. With the aid of two big burly asylum attendants, Mrs Wilson was eventually got into a backyard ... and later by a successful police manoeuvre she was removed from danger.[70]

In February 1908, Lavena Saltonstall was the only one of the Halifax women to answer the WSPU call to go down to London for another march on Parliament. After the recent frightening events at Lancaster, and taking into consideration Willson's having 'looked ill' when imprisoned in Holloway, it would be no surprise if her husband had begged her to remain at home.

Saltonstall was arrested again and imprisoned in Holloway – this time for six weeks. Saltonstall was younger than the other women and had no family commitments at home. This didn't necessarily make more than a month in cold, forbidding conditions any easier, but she kept her spirits up by writing spirited and fiery letters to the press.

Saltonstall was released on 19 March. A gathering was arranged in George Square to welcome her home, with Mrs Willson leading the speakers. Once again, violence flared. A number of youths began to interrupt Mrs Willson, with cries such as, 'Go hoam and mend your husband's socks.' There were 'ugly scrimmages', and the crowd rushed the women, nearly knocking Mrs Willson down, before kicking Saltonstall brutally. Willson was advised to break up the meeting after the youths began to throw missiles, but they were followed as they left by 'hundreds of youths'.[71]

Laura Willson c. 1920 (Family archive CC BY SA 4.0)

It's worth noting that at this time, more than a year after Pankhurst had given a rousing speech in Hebden Bridge, hundreds of fustian weavers in the town had still seen no settlement to their strike. It was also only just over a year since the tram workers' strike had ended in ignominious defeat and the loss of many jobs. Feelings in Halifax were almost certainly still running high, and it's possible that many were taking it out on the suffragettes.

With the constant threat of violence, and the split in the party in London causing many to question

Pankhurst's leadership and militant tactics, it's no surprise that from this year the Halifax women's activity in direct suffragette action slowed. The women also had family commitments. Dinah Connelly had a third baby in 1909, and Laura Willson a second baby in 1911. However, they continued to be passionately behind the votes for women movement.

Halifax Suffragettes and the Boycott of the 1911 Census

In March 1911, Emmeline Pankhurst was again back in Halifax to speak to a packed meeting at the Mechanics' Institute. Her topic this time was the 'No vote, no census' campaign, and she gave a typically rousing speech. Suffrage campaigners planned to boycott the census as a protest, either by remaining away from home and avoiding the census altogether, or by defacing their entry. Protesters risked a fine or even imprisonment.

The meeting at the Mechanics' Institute was chaired by Dr Helena Jones, who had moved to Halifax from Kings Norton. Dr Jones was an active member of the WSPU before moving to the town, and in 1911 she was secretary of the Halifax WSPU branch. Laura Willson had stepped down and appears to have been much less active within the WSPU. It is possible the violence she had encountered and her spells in prison had taken their toll. It's also possible she didn't agree with the WSPU's increasingly militant tactics. In addition, her baby had been born at the beginning of 1911, and the new arrival must surely have taken up much of her time. Whatever the case, Laura Willson took no steps either to deface or to avoid the census, and she and the rest of her family are listed as living at 117 Beechwood Road, Illingworth.

Willson's great friend, Dinah Connelly, is listed with her family at 22 Howard Street. Connelly didn't boycott the census, but she listed her occupation as 'Slave'. Mary Taylor lived at 32 Skircoat Green Road. She appears to have boycotted the census – the only occupant listed in the house in 1911 was her husband, Arthur. Lavena Saltonstall is not listed in the 1911 census, and she also appears to have successfully boycotted it.

In 1911, the new WSPU secretary, Dr Jones, was living at Rhodesia Avenue, Savile Park. The census lists only her housekeeper, who declared that the head of the household was not present on the night of the census, and that she didn't return until after 8 a.m. the following morning.

These are the names of Halifax suffragettes that we can now look up and find (or not) in the 1911 census. When it comes to other census entries in Halifax that year, it's much more difficult after a hundred years to establish motives and reasons for a woman not appearing on the census entry for her home.

In 1911, the census had additional columns which recorded, for the first time, the number of years a woman had been married, plus her 'Total Children Born Alive', 'Children still Living', and 'Children who have Died'. These columns went against the wife's entry, and not the husband's. We can only imagine how distressing this question must have been for women whose children had died. As we have seen, 1909 had seen the end of the Mayor of Halifax's 'Baby Bounty' scheme, when women whose babies survived their first year were rewarded with a sovereign. In 1911, this insensitivity to women's (and men's) grief was being carried out on a national scale.

Kathleen Wilson, the first female employee at the Halifax Building Society, lived with her parents and her older brother, an electrical engineer, at 325 Skircoat Green Road – the same road as suffragette Mary Taylor. On the night of the 1911 census, Kathleen's mother, Florence, was absent from the home. Because of the intrusive nature of the new questions, the 'No vote, No census' campaign had received support from many women. That night, Florence Wilson is recorded as being at the house of her older sister, Fanny, who lived near Warley Road. Fanny was married to George Hebblethwaite, a man of 'independent means'. Fanny and George lived in a large house with their three children, along with a 17-year-old servant, as well as Florence and Fanny's 86-year-old mother. Why would Florence stay overnight on census night, away from her own husband and children, when the families lived so close? It is possible that her elderly mother was ill, but even then, an overnight stay would not have been necessary, with Florence's sister and a servant there to look after her. Florence's name has been added in a slightly different ink at the bottom of the other census entries for the household. Florence had had four children. It is recorded that two of them were dead. It's possible Florence hadn't wanted to have this information recorded, or even to be reminded of it, and so had gone to her sister's to avoid having to answer the questions. If so, it's also possible that George Hebblethwaite insisted or persuaded Florence to obey the law and to record her presence as a visitor.

Because of the nature of the 1911 census protest, of course it is now not possible to analyse the census with accuracy. Florence Wilson's reason for being absent from her own home is a mystery, but it's also her private mystery to keep.

Votes for Women

With the outbreak of the First World War, Emmeline Pankhurst and the WSPU agreed to cease their militant activities.

Prior to the war, because of the property laws, only sixty-three per cent of men had the vote in Britain. No women had the vote. The war changed everything. Women were stepping into the workplace in their thousands, proving irrevocably that they could do the same jobs as the men. Millions of men who were not eligible to vote were sent to fight for their country by those who were.

On 6 February 1918, the Representation of the People Act enfranchised more than five million men over the age of 21, without regard to property or class. Eight million women over 30 who held property, or whose husbands held property, were also given the right to vote.

It wasn't until 2 July 1928, and the Equal Franchise Act, that women finally gained what the suffragettes had been fighting for for a quarter of a century – the same voting rights as men. Sadly, Emmeline Pankhurst died just a few weeks before the Act was passed, on 14 June 1928.

Of the Halifax suffragettes, Lavena Saltonstall continued her education, joining classes at the Workers' Education Association in Halifax when it formed in 1909. In June 1917 she married Private George Moore Baker.[72]

In 1920, Mary Taylor – who had been imprisoned for refusing to accept the legality of a court run solely by men – was appointed one of the first three women magistrates in Halifax.

As noted in the chapter on women in employment, Laura Annie Willson was awarded a MBE for her services to munition workers in the First World War. Willson set up her own building business, founded the Women's Engineering Society, and in 1927, having moved south from Halifax with her husband, she began her trade as a builder in Surrey.

In 1912, Dinah Connelly had a baby girl. Laura Annie Connelly later married Walter Mitchell and, as Laura Mitchell, in 1967 she became Mayor of Halifax.

The Laura Mitchell Health Centre provides a vital service in Halifax – including the provision of family planning advice to all. The centre is named after Dinah Connelly's daughter. Dinah Connelly named her daughter after her great friend, Laura Annie Willson. It is hugely satisfying to know that the memories of these Halifax women live on in this way in the town today.

Bibliography

Books

Akroyd, Edward *On the Plan of Juvenile and Adult Education Adopted in the Writer's Manufactory* (London 1857)

Anderson, Gregory *White Blouse Revolution: Female Office Workers since 1870* (Manchester University Press 1989)

Bates, Denise *Pit Lasses: Women and Girls in Coalmining c. 1800-1914* (Wharncliffe Books 2012)

Bentley, Phyllis *"O Dreams, O Destinations": The Autobiography of Phyllis Bentley* (Gollancz 1962)

Binns, Amy *Valley of a Hundred Chapels* (Grace Judson Press 2013)

Cox, Thomas *The Grammar School of Queen Elizabeth at Heath nr Halifax* 1879

Chase, Malcolm *Chartism: A New History* (Manchester University Press 2007)

Crawford, Elizabeth *The Women's Suffrage Movement: A Reference Guide 1866-1928* (Routledge 2003)

Crawford, Elizabeth *The Women's Suffrage Movement in Britain and Ireland: A Regional Survey* (Routledge 2006)

Davis, Sam and Morley, Bob *County Borough Elections in England and Wales, 1919–1938 Volume 4: Exeter – Hull* (Routledge 2013)

Driver, Cecil *Tory Radical: The Life of Richard Oastler* (New York, 1946)

Duffield, Margaret *From Cobbles, Candles and Clogs* (Sephton Enterprise Publications 2001)

Ginswick, Jules *Labour and the Poor in England and Wales – Letters to the Morning Chronicle Volume I: Lancashire, Cheshire, Yorkshire 1849 – 1851* (Routledge 1983)

Gomersall, Meg *Working-Class Girls in Nineteenth Century England* (Macmillan Press 1997)

Grundy, Francis *Pictures of the Past* (Griffith and Farran 1879)

Hanson, T. W. *The Story of Old Halifax* (F. King & Sons Ltd 1920)

Hargreaves, John *Halifax* (Edinburgh University Press 1999)

Hinton, James *Women, Social Leadership, and the Second World War* (OUP 2002)

Hobson, O. R. *100 Years of the Halifax* (Batsford 1953)

Howe, Catherine *Halifax 1842: A Year of Crisis* (Breviary Stuff 2014)

Hutchins, B.L. *Women in Modern Industry* (G. Bell and Sons 1915)

Liddington, Jill *Female Fortune: Land, Gender and Authority* (Rivers Oram Press 1998)

Liddington, Jill *Rebel Girls: How Votes for Women Changed Edwardian Lives* (Virago 2015)

Liddington, Jill and Norris, Jill *One Hand Tied Behind Us: Rise of the Women's Suffrage Movement* (Rivers Oram Press 2000)

Mulvihill, Margaret *Charlotte Despard: A Biography* (Pandora Press 1989)

Pankhurst, Emmeline *My Own Story* (Project Gutenberg First published 1914)

Peel, Frank *The Risings of the Luddites, Chartists and Plug-Drawers* (Frank Cass & Co 1968)

Priestley, J. B. *Margin Released* (Heron Books 1962)

Roth, H. Ling *Yorkshire Coiners* (F. King and Sons 1906)

Schroeder, Mary *A Halifax Childhood* (Erskine Press 2004)

Smith, Barbara Leigh *A Brief Study in Plain Language of the Most Important Laws Concerning Women* (Holyoake and Co, 1856)

Steedman, Carolyn *Master and Servant: Love and Labour in the English Industrial Age* (Cambridge University Press 2007)

Steinbach, Susie *Women in England 1760 – 1914* (Orion Books 2005)

Taylor, Rose; Kafel, Andrew and Smith, Russell *Crossley Heath School* (The History Press 2006)

Thomas, Peter *Seeing It Through – Halifax & Calderdale During World War II* (Peter Thomas 2005)

Thompson, Dorothy *The Early Chartists* (Macmillan 1971)

Thompson, E.P. *Customs in Common* (Penguin 1993)

Thornton, Joan *It Were No Laughing Matter* (Yorkshire Art Circus 1987)

Whitbread, Helena *I Know My Own Heart: The Diaries of Anne Lister, 1791-1840* (Virago Press 1988)

Whitbread, Helena *No Priest But Love: The Journals of Anne Lister from 1824-1826* (New York University Press 1993)

Pamphlets, Documents, Articles and Media

Askwith, Eveline *Parlourmaid to Housekeeper* (C. R. Eastwood, Somerset, 2003)

Baylis, Thomas Henry *The Rights, Duties and Relations of Domestic Servants and their Masters and Mistresses* (Oxford University Library 1857)

Bodichon, Barbara L. S. *A Brief Summary in Plain Language of the Most Important Laws Concerning Women* (1869 Trubner & Co)

Cockcroft, Janet *Not a Proper Doctor: The Life and Times of an Off-Cumden in Halifax* (Pennine Heritage 1986)

Cookson, Dr Gillian *Women and Children in the Card-Making Industry in Halifax and West Yorkshire* (Recording, 2nd October 1999 HAS ref (B)B:13:1#)

Crabtree, George *A Brief Description of a Tour through Calder Dale* (Calderdale Libraries P331CRA)

Dale, Pamela and Fisher, Kate *Contrasting Municipal Responses to the Provision of Birth Control Services in Halifax and Exeter before 1948* (Social History of Medicine, Volume 23, Issue 3, 1 December 2010, Pages 567–585)

Defoe, Daniel *A Tour Thro' the whole Island of Great Britain Vol 2* (reprinted 1927 Calderdale Libraries Doc ID: 100801)

Goldthorpe, Leslie *Fustian Weavers' Strike Hebden Bridge 1906–1908* (Hebden Bridge Literary and Scientific Society, Local History Booklet, No 3. 1982)

Greg, William *Why Are Women Redundant?* 1869

Haugh Shaw School Centenary Brochure 1879-1979 (Calderdale Library Archives)

Holton, Sandra Stanley *Friendship and Domestic Service: the letters of Eliza Oldham, general maid (c.1820–1892)* Women's History Review 2015, 24:3, 429-449, DOI: 10.1080/09612025.2014.975498

Humphreys, Rita *Rita's Story* (Purnell Secretarial Services, Bridgwater, 1992)

King, R. T. *A History of St Augustine's Schools* 1868-1968 (Calderdale Library Archives)

Liddington, Jill *Gender, authority and mining in an industrial landscape: Anne Lister 1791-1840* (History Workshop Journal, Volume 1996, Issue 42, 1 January 1996, Pages 59–86)

Long, Vicky and Marland, Hilary *From Danger and Motherhood to Health and Beauty: Health Advice for the Factory Girl in Early Twentieth-Century Britain.* (20 Century British History 2009, 20(4), 454–481)

Roth, H. Ling *Hand Card Making* (Bankfield Museum Notes 1910)

Sykes, Mary *40 Years On* (Barden Print Ltd)

Walker, Selwyn Joseph Sykes *The History of Joseph Sykes Brothers 1937 – 1939, updated 1976* (Huddersfield Library Archives)

White's History, Gazetteer and Directory of the West-Riding of Yorkshire 1837 (original document digitised and available from Google Books)

Wilson, Benjamin *The Struggles of an Old Chartist* 1886 (Calderdale Libraries ref. 13960019)

Whiteley, David *The Story of the Halifax Sunday School Jubilees* 1912 (Calderdale Library Archives)

Official programme of the Halifax Sunday School Union 1913 (Calderdale Library Archives)

Married and Single Ladies' Entertainment Programme (Roomfield Baptist Church, Todmorden, 1908)

Princess Mary's School Brochure 1954 (Calderdale Library Archives)

Colden School Centenary Brochure 1878 – 1978 (Calderdale Library Archives)

Crossley's Carpets Centenary Brochure 1903

Round the Table – Halifax Permanent Benefit Building Society Staff magazine. Various years. (Lloyds Banking Group Archives)

Wings Newsletter Oct 1900 (Calderdale Library Archives)

Halifax Antiquarian Society Transactions

Akroyd, Jean Mallinson *A Country Childhood* 2008

Green, E. P. *The Brooksbank School* 1964

Laybourn, Keith *The New Philanthropy of the Edwardian Age: The Guild of Help and the Halifax Citizens' Guild, 1905–1918* 2015

Webster, Eric *Halifax Schools 1870–1970* 1972

Government Reports

Report of the Select Committee on Factory Children's Labour (Parliamentary Papers 1831–32, volume XV)

Factories Inquiry Commission: Supplementary Report as to the Employment of Children in Factories, and as to the Propriety and Means of Curtailing the Hours of Their Labour 1834, Volume 2

Return of the Number of Persons Employed in Cotton, Woollen, Worsted, Flax and Silk Factories of the United Kingdom XLV 1836

Reports from Commissioners (Inspectors of Factories) Vol X 1841

The Children's Employment Commission (Mines) Report 1842

William Ranger's Report to the General Board of Health (Halifax) 1851

Schools Inquiry Commission Report Volume I 1867-8

Schools Inquiry Commission Vol. IX General Reports by Assistant Commissioners 1868

Schools Inquiry Commission Vol. XVIII Yorkshire 1868

Report to the Royal Commission on Labour on the Employment of Women 9th May 1892

Annual Report of King Edward VII Memorial District Nursing Association 1929 – 30

Reports of the Chief Medical Officer of Health for Halifax 1918, 1921, 1934, 1935, 1936, 1948, 1950, 1951

County Borough of Halifax Proposals for Carrying out Duties under Sections 22-29 of the NHS Act, 1946 1948

Academic Documents

McDowell, Carina *Staffing the Big House: Country House Domestic Service in Yorkshire 1800-1903* (MA Thesis, University of Ottawa 2012)

Plant, Helen *Gender and the aristocracy of Dissent: a comparative study of the beliefs, status and roles of women in Quaker and Unitarian communities, 1770–1830, with particular reference to Yorkshire* (Submitted for the degree of DPhil. University of York 2000)

Websites

Mount Zion Methodist Heritage Chapel: http://www.mountzionhalifax.org.uk/

Malcolm Bull's Calderdale Companion: www.calderdalecompanion.co.uk

Denise Bates (author of *Pit Lasses*): www.denisebates.co.uk

The Children's Home: http://www.childrenshomes.org.uk/list/MH11.shtml

Ruth Skyte *Our Family*: http://www.rijo.homepage.t-online.de/pdf/en_de_ju_sky50132.pdf

Royal Voluntary Service Archive https://www.royalvoluntaryservice.org.uk/about-us/our-history/archive-online/voices-of-volunteering

Joseph Crossley Homes http://josephcrossleyhomes.org.uk/the-almshouses-1/

Citations

Child Labour and Girls at Work

Girls at Work in the Card-Making Industry

1. Daniel Defoe *Tour Thro' the whole Island of Great Britain Vol 2*
2. Selwyn Walker *The History of Joseph Sykes Brothers*
3. Ibid.
4. H. Ling Roth *Hand Card Making*
5. *White's History Gazetteer and Directory of the West-Riding 1837* p.399
6. Selwyn Joseph Sykes Walker *The History of Joseph Sykes Brothers 1937–1939*

Girls at Work in the Textile Mills

7. Quoted in Cecil Driver *Tory Radical* p.50
8. Ibid. p.52
9. Report of the Commissioners on the employment of children in factories (1833), quoted in T. W. Hanson *The Story of Old Halifax* p.244
10. T. W. Hanson *The Story of Old Halifax* p.243
11. *Halifax and Huddersfield Express* 12.3.1831
12. Letter to the *Leeds Intelligencer*, quoted in Cecil Driver *Tory Radical* p.76.
13. Ibid. p.198
14. *Report of the Select Committee on Factory Children's Labour 1831-32 volume XV* p.28
15. *Factories Inquiry Commission, Supplementary Report as to the Employment of Children in Factories 1834 vol II* p.63

16. Ibid. p.280
17. George Crabtree *A Brief Description of a Tour through Calder Dale* p.12
18. Ibid. pp.13-14
19. Ibid. p.25
20. *Bradford Observer* 1.12.1842
21. *The Morning Post* 27.4.1832
22. *Hull Packet and Humber Mercury* 1.5.1832
23. Cecil Driver *Tory Radical* p.159
24. T. W. Hanson *The Story of Old Halifax* p.244

Girls at Work in the Mines

25. *The Children's Employment Commission (Mines) 1842 Report* p.141
26. *Leeds Mercury* 7.7.1838
27. Advertisement quoted in Malcolm Bull's Calderdale Companion
28. *The Children's Employment Commission (Mines) 1842 Report* p.4
29. Ibid. p.80
30. Ibid. p.80
31. Anne Lister's Diary, quoted in Jill Liddington *Gender, authority and mining in an industrial landscape*
32. Ibid.
33. Ibid.
34. Ibid.
35. Information on Patience's life: website of Denise Bates. Asylum records: West Yorkshire Archives WYAS C85/3/6/20/p333A-333B/1

An Unequal Education

The Early Years

1. *Official Programme of the Sunday School Union* 1913
2. Mount Zion website

3. David Whiteley *The Story of the Halifax Sunday School Jubilees*
4. *Married and Single Ladies' Entertainment Programme* Roomfield Baptist Church, Todmorden, March 1908, quoted in Amy Binns *Valley of a Hundred Chapels* p.69
5. *Official Programme of the Sunday School Union* 1913
6. Helena Whitbread *I Know My Own Heart* p.227
7. Anne Lister's diaries can be read in Helena Whitbread's *I Know My Own Heart* and *No Priest But Love*
8. *Leeds Mercury* 1.5.1868
9. *Wings Newsletter* Oct 1900
10. *Schools Inquiry Commission Vol. XVIII* 1868 p.248
11. *Leeds Mercury* 21.1.1874
12. Eric Webster *Halifax Schools 1870-1970* HAS 1972
13. John Hargreaves *Halifax* p.152
14. R. T. King *History of St Augustine's Schools*

'A cruel injustice.' The Schools Inquiry Commission 1867-68

15. Ibid.
16. H. Ling Roth *Yorkshire Coiners* p.48
17. *Schools Inquiry Commission Vol. IX* 1868 p.337
18. Ibid. p.281
19. Malcolm Bull's Calderdale Companion
20. *Schools Inquiry Commission Vol. IX* 1868 p.288
21. Ibid. p.363
22. Ibid. p.195
23. Malcolm Bull's Calderdale Companion
24. E. P. Green *The Brooksbank School* HAS Transactions 1964 p.36
25. *Schools Inquiry Commission Vol. IX* 1868 p.380
26. Ibid. p.140
27. Ibid. p.363
28. *Leeds Mercury* 22.10.1870
29. *Leeds Mercury* 8.2.1879
30. *Leeds Mercury* 5.2.1876

31. *Leeds Mercury* 1.2.1878
32. Phyllis Bentley *"O Dreams, O Destinations"* p.65
33. Ibid. p.65
34. *Halifax Girls' Secondary School magazine* 1931

The Focus on Domestic Science

35. *Halifax Courier and Guardian* 16.12.1939
36. Quoted in Carina McDowell *Staffing the Big House* p.44
37. Taylor, Kafel and Smith *Crossley Heath School* p.39
38. Ibid. p.49
39. *Halifax Courier* 29.7.1939
40. Rita Humphreys *Rita's Story* p.34
41. *Halifax Courier* 18.7.2009

Further Education: the Halifax girls 'not burdened with a serious education'

42. Helena Whitbread *I Know My Own Heart* p.43
43. Ibid. p.39
44. Helen Plant *Gender and the aristocracy of Dissent*
45. Helena Whitbread *I Know My Own Heart* p.143
46. Jill Liddington *Female Fortune: Land, Gender and Authority* p.45
47. *Leeds Mercury* 22.4.1865
48. Edward Akroyd *On the Plan of Juvenile and Adult Education Adopted in the Writer's Manufactory* p.269
49. *Bradford Observer* 11.4.1861
50. *Leeds Mercury* 21.12.1872
51. *Schools Inquiry Commission Vol. IX* 1868 p.380
52. Janet Cockcroft *Not a Proper Doctor* p. 13
53. Ibid. p.17
54. Phyllis Bentley *"O dreams, O destinations"* p.87
55. Ibid. p.113
56. John Hargreaves *Halifax* p.118
57. Princess Mary's School Brochure 1954

Women's Health and Domestic Lives

Women's Chores in the Home

1. T. W. Hanson *The Story of Old Halifax* p.262
2. Ibid. p.262
3. *William Ranger's Report to the General Board of Health (Halifax)* 1851 p.17
4. Quoted in O.R. Hobson *100 Years of the Halifax* p.152
5. *Women's Trade Union Review* 11.11.1904, quoted in Liddington/Norris *One Hand Tied Behind Us* p.15
6. Joan Thornton *It Were No Laughing Matter* p.25
7. *Yorkshire Evening Post* 28.2.1928
8. M. Gomersall *Working-Class Girls in Nineteenth Century England* p.24
9. Mary Schroeder *A Halifax Childhood* p.47
10. Phyllis Bentley *"O Dreams, O Destinations"* p.272

Courtship and Marriage

11. Helena Whitbread *I Know My Own Heart* p.312
12. *York Herald* 29.11.1823
13. Jill Liddington *Rebel Girls* p.83
14. Barbara L. S. Bodichon *A Brief Summary in Plain Language of the Most Important Laws Concerning Women* p.4
15. Helena Whitbread *I Know My Own Heart* p.92
16. *Halifax Courier* 27.1.1855
17. E. P. Thompson *Customs in Common* p.409
18. Helena Whitbread *I Know My Own Heart* p.323
19. E. P. Thompson *Customs in Common* p.410
20. *The Northern Star and Leeds General Advertiser* 21.4.1838
21. Mary Schroeder *A Halifax Childhood* p.72

Sexual Abuse and Harassment

22. Helena Whitbread *I Know My Own Heart* p.128
23. Ibid. p.129
24. *Halifax Courier* 6.8.1853

25. *Halifax Courier* 15.2.1868
26. *Halifax Courier* 18.2.1854
27. Rita Humphreys *Rita's Story* p.44
28. *Bradford Observer* 13.10.1859
29. *Report to the Royal Commission on Labour on the Employment of Women* 1892
30. J. B. Priestley *Margin Released* p.199
31. *Halifax Courier* 18.2.1939

Pregnancy and Childbirth

32. Janet Cockcroft *Not a Proper Doctor* p.11
33. Margaret Duffield *From Cobbles, Candles and Clogs* p.35
34. *Todmorden Advertiser and Hebden Bridge Newsletter* 10.1.1908
35. *Leeds Mercury* 12.2.1909
36. *Halifax Courier* 20.3.1953
37. Annual Report of King Edward VII Memorial District Nursing Association 1929 – 30
38. Phyllis Bentley *"O Dreams, O Destinations"* p.115

Birth Control

39. *Bradford Observer* 27.2.1862
40. Margaret Duffield *From Cobbles, Candles and Clogs* p.79
41. Rita Humphreys *Rita's Story* p.56
42. *Yorkshire Post and Leeds Intelligencer* 2.5.1949
43. *Halifax Courier*14.1939
44. *County Borough of Halifax Proposals for Carrying out Duties under Sections 22-29 of the NHS Act, 1946* 1948
45. *Report of the Chief Medical Officer of Health* 1950
46. Heinz and Thea Ruth Skyte *Our Family*
47. *Report of the Chief Medical Officer of Health* 1948
48. *Halifax Courier* 4.4.2007
49. *Leeds Mercury* 12.7.1922
50. *Leeds Mercury* 23.2.1934
51. Janet Cockcroft *Not a Proper Doctor* p.38
52. WWC minutes 6.11.1934 (WYAS CC00258 MISC:190)

53. Ibid. 11.3.1936 (WYAS CC00258 MISC:190)
54. Ibid. 11.3.1936 (WYAS CC00258 MISC:190)
55. *Report of the Chief Medical Officer of Health* 1934 and 1935
56. Battinson Rd School Brochure 1937
57. Janet Cockcroft *Not a Proper Doctor* p.46

Women in Employment

What Did Middle-Class Women Do?

1. Long and Marland *From Danger and Motherhood to Health and Beauty*
2. Helena Whitbread *I Know My Own Heart* p.117
3. *Pall Mall Gazette* 24.10.1898
4. Jill Liddington *Female Fortune: Land, Gender and Authority* p. 66
5. Helena Whitbread *I Know My Own Heart* p.49
6. Ibid. p.44
7. Phyllis Bentley *"O Dreams, O Destinations"* p.81
8. Ibid. p.106
9. Ibid. p.106
10. *Leeds Mercury* 2.6.1870
11. Phyllis Bentley *"O Dreams, O Destinations"* p.107
12. Ibid. p.82
13. Ibid. p.169
14. Janet Cockcroft *Not a Proper Doctor* p.22
15. Ibid. p.23
16. *Bradford & Wakefield Observer* 1.4.1847
17. *Leeds Mercury* 29.3.1851
18. *Leeds Mercury* 16.9.1820
19. Keith Laybourn *The New Philanthropy of the Edwardian Age 1905–1918* HAS 2015
20. Janet Cockcroft *Not a Proper Doctor* p.38
21. Sam Davis and Bob Morley *County Borough Elections in England and Wales, 1919–1938 Volume 4: Exeter – Hull* p.360
22. *Halifax Courier* 5.8.1939
23. *Halifax Courier* 3.3.1939

24. *Halifax Courier* 29.4.1939
25. James Hinton *Women, Social Leadership, and the Second World War: Continuities of Class* p.190
26. *Halifax Courier* 4.3.1939
27. Royal Voluntary Service website, Voices of Volunteering, Interview ref: Higg
28. *Yorkshire Post* 25.4.1945

Working-Class Women and Their Jobs

29. *Halifax Courier* 4.3.1939
30. Margaret Duffield *From Cobbles, Candles and Clogs* p.17
31. Mary Sykes *40 Years On* p.23
32. Joan Thornton *It Were No Laughing Matter* p.104
33. *Yorkshire Evening Post* 17.7.1948
34. *Yorkshire Post* 17.8.1948

Women in Domestic Service

35. John Hargreaves *Halifax* p.137
36. Carina MacDowell *Staffing the Big House* p.14
37. Letter to Helen Clark 1st December 1890, quoted in Sandra Stanley Holton *Friendship and Domestic Service*
38. Helena Whitbread *I Know My Own Heart* p.127
39. Anne Lister to Ann Lister 13.9.1828, quoted in Carina MacDowell *Staffing the Big House*
40. Helena Whitbread *No Priest But Love* p.38
41. Anne Lister 1 October 1828, quoted in Carina MacDowell *Staffing the Big House*
42. Helena Whitbread *I Know My Own Heart* p.42
43. Mary Schroeder *A Halifax Childhood* p.43
44. Eveline Askwith *From Parlourmaid to Housekeeper* p.19
45. Ibid. p.12
46. Joseph Crossley Homes website
47. Eveline Askwith *From Parlourmaid to Housekeeper* p.32
48. Rita Humphreys *Rita's Story* p.10
49. Ibid. p.11
50. Ibid. p.12

Women at Work in the Mills, Factories and Engineering

51. George Crabtree *A Brief Description of a Tour through Calder Dale* p.1
52. Susie Steinbach *Women in England* p.22
53. *The Spectator* 11.5.1844
54. Angus Reach quoted in Jules Ginswick *Labour and the Poor in England and Wales – Letters to the Morning Chronicle Volume I 1849–1851* pp.170-72
55. *Leeds Mercury* 14.9.1922
56. *Crossley's Carpets Centenary Brochure* 1903
57. 17.3.1870, Crossley Archives C300/B8/1 WYAS Wakefield
58. *Report to the Royal Commission on Labour on the Employment of Women* 1892
59. Ibid.
60. *Yorkshire Post* 19.6.1947
61. *Yorkshire Post* 30.6.1947
62. Ibid.
63. John Hargreaves *Halifax* p.122
64. Sheffield Daily Telegraph 16.9.1921
65. *Yorkshire Post* 28.4.1913
66. *Reports from Commissioners (Inspectors of Factories) Appendix I Vol X* 1841
67. *Bradford Observer* 19.12.1850
68. *Bradford Observer* 9.2.1860
69. John Hargreaves *Halifax* p.121
70. *Yorkshire Post* 23.3.1920
71. *Leeds Mercury* 4.9.1926
72. *Yorkshire Post* 4.9.1926
73. *Yorkshire Post* 25.2.1927
74. *Leeds Mercury* 25.8.1917

The Halifax Building Society: 'No Female Shall Be Admitted to Any Office Therein'

75. John Hargreaves *Halifax* p. 123
76. *Halifax Courier* 10.1.1914
77. O.R. Hobson *A Hundred Years of the Halifax* p.26

78. *Halifax Permanent Benefit Building Society Annual Report* 1918
79. *Round the Table* 1917
80. Ibid
81. Report of the Halifax AGM in *Round the Table* 1918
82. *Halifax Courier* 5.8.1939
83. *Round the Table* May 1927
84. *Round the Table* November 1956
85. O. R. Hobson *A Hundred Years of the Halifax* Appendix XI
86. Quoted in Gregory Anderson *White Blouse Revolution: Female Office Workers since 1870* p.63

Chartism, Radical Politics, and Votes for Women

Halifax Women and Nineteenth Century Radical Politics

1. Helena Whitbread *I Know My Own Heart* p.109
2. Benjamin Wilson *The Struggles of an Old Chartist p.1*
3. T.W. Hanson *The Story of Old Halifax* p.252
4. Ibid. p.250
5. Benjamin Wilson *The Struggles of an Old Chartist p.2*
6. T.W. Hanson *The Story of Old Halifax* p.252
7. Helena Whitbread *I Know My Own Heart* p.108
8. Jill Liddington *Female Fortune: Land, Gender and Authority* p.45
9. Benjamin Wilson *Struggles of an Old Chartist* p.3
10. *Leeds Times* 17.2.1838
11. *Northern Star* 24.3.1838
12. Dorothy Thompson *The Early Chartists* p.87
13. *Northern Star* 9.6.1838
14. Benjamin Wilson *Struggles of an Old Chartist* p.4
15. Quoted in Catherine Howe *Halifax 1842* p.77
16. T.W. Hanson *The Story of Old Halifax* p.256
17. *Bradford Observer* 18.8.1842
18. Frank Peel *The Risings of the Luddites, Chartists and Plug-Drawers* p.340
19. Ibid. p.341

20. Francis Grundy *Pictures of the Past* p.99
21. *York Herald* 20.8.1842
22. *Bradford Observer* 18.8.1842
23. *Northern Star* 28.8.1847
24. Benjamin Wilson *Struggles of an Old Chartist* p.10
25. From G. D. H. Cole *Chartist Portraits*, quoted in Catherine Howe *Halifax 1842* p.139
26. Elizabeth Crawford *The Women's Suffrage Movement: A Reference Guide* p.48

The Halifax Suffragettes

27. *Bradford Observer* 6.1.1874
28. Elizabeth Crawford *The Women's Suffrage Movement in Britain and Ireland* p.48
29. Susie Steinbach *Women in England* p.302
30. Emmeline Pankhurst *My Own Story*
31. *Todmorden Advertiser and Hebden Bridge Newsletter* 4.8.1905
32. Jill Liddington *Rebel Girls* p.90
33. Ibid. p.90
34. *Leeds Mercury* 16.4.1906
35. *Bradford Daily Telegraph* 2.7.1906
36. *Halifax Guardian* 11.8.1906, quoted in Jill Liddington *Rebel Girls* p.90
37. *Leeds Mercury* 27.8.1906
38. *Bradford Daily Telegraph* 1.9.1906
39. *Todmorden & District News* 7.9.1906
40. *Leeds Mercury* 14.9.1906
41. Jill Liddington *Rebel Girls* p.92
42. *Todmorden & District News* 21.9.1906
43. *Leeds Mercury* 22.9.1906
44. *Halifax Evening Courier* 17.10.1906, quoted in Jill Liddington *Rebel Girls* p.93
45. Jill Liddington *Rebel Girls* p.96
46. *Todmorden and District News* 1.2.1907

47. *Todmorden Advertiser and Hebden Bridge Newsletter* 1.2.1907
48. *Todmorden and District News* 1.2.1907
49. *Todmorden Advertiser and Hebden Bridge Newsletter* 1.2.1907
50. Jill Liddington *Rebel Girls* p.101
51. *Leeds Mercury* 21.2.1907
52. *Todmorden Advertiser* 22.2.1907
53. *Hull Daily Mail* 21.2.1907
54. *Todmorden Advertiser* 1.3.1907
55. Leslie Goldthorpe *Fustian Weavers' Strike Hebden Bridge 1906-1908*
56. *Sheffield Daily Telegraph* 21.3.1907
57. *Leeds Mercury* 15.2.1907
58. *Shipley Times and Express* 15.2.1907
59. *Leeds Mercury* 21.2.1907
60. *Leeds Mercury* 4.3.1907
61. *Sheffield Evening Telegraph* 20.3.1907
62. *Leeds Mercury* 4.4.1907
63. *Leeds Mercury* 25.1.1907
64. *Hull Daily Mail* 20.1.1908
65. *Sheffield Daily Telegraph* 20.1.1908
66. Alice Milne's diaries, quoted in Margaret Mulvihill *Charlotte Despard* p.81
67. Report to the Women's Freedom League 12.10.1907, quoted in Jill Liddington *Rebel Girls* p.166
68. *Yorkshire Evening Post* 5.12.1907
69. *Sheffield Daily Telegraph* 16.1.1908
70. *Manchester Courier and Lancashire General Advertiser* 17.1.1908
71. *Bradford Daily Telegraph* 23.3.1908
72. Jill Liddington *Rebel Girls* p.190

Index

Abortion, 72, 78–9, 86
    various pills for, 77
        see also birth control
Accidents in the workplace
    s*ee* Health and Safety
Adoption, 82–3
    see also Saint Margaret's
        House
Akroyd, Edward:
    mill schools, 29
    Halifax Working Men's
        College, 47
    Halifax Young Women's
        Institute, 47
Akroyd, James, 8, 14, 15
    factory owners' meeting,
        Old Cock Inn, 9–10,
        130
    Old Lane Mill, 12–13, 114
    death of, 17
    plug riots, 144
        see also equal pay
Akroyd, Jonathan, 17
Anti-Corn Law League
    see voluntary work
Anti-Slavery movement
    see voluntary work
Arkwright, Richard, 3
Askwith, Eveline, 107–108

Baby Bounty Scheme, 73, 172
Baines, Jennie, 160, 169

Balfour Education Act
    (1902), 31
Band of Hope, 64–5
Battinson Road School, 87
Bazaars
    see Voluntary work
Beacon Club, the
    see voluntary work
Beale, Dorothy, 32
Beatson, Phoebe, 104
Becker, Lydia, 149
Benefits
    see Welfare
Bentley, Phyllis:
    further education, 49, 91
    Halifax Girls' High
        School, 37–9
    voluntary work, 74–5, 99
    war work (munitions),
    91–2
    writing, 93
        see also housework
Billington-Greig, Teresa, 167
Birth control, 72, 77
    Family Planning Clinic,
        93
    Municipal Birth Control
        Clinic, Northgate 85,
        87
    National Birth Control
        Association, 84
    voices against, 84

see also abortion
see also Women's Welfare
    Clinic
Blakey, Esther
    see Voluntary work
Blue Coats School, 43–4
Bright, John, 103
British School, 29–30

Calderdale College
    see Halifax Technical
        College
Carding, 1–3, 114
carding machine, 3, 113
Card-setting, 1–6
    setting schools, 4
Charity schools, 19–20
Charity work
    see Voluntary work
Chew, Ada Nield, 53
Childbirth
    see pregnancy
Churchill, Winston, 151–2
Clay, Mrs Howard, 39
Cockcroft, Dr Janet, 71, 73,
    100
    Education, 48–9, 73–4, 93
    Family Planning Clinic,
        93
    National Council of
        Women (NCW), 96–7,
        98
    Women's Welfare Clinic
        (WWC), 85, 88
Connelly, Dinah, 152, 162,
    163, 165–6, 171, 174
Corn Laws, 14–15

Anti-Corn Law League
    see voluntary work
Corporal punishment, 7–8,
    12, 21, 29
Council elections *see* elections
Crabtree, George, 12–14, 110
Crossley's Carpets, 70, 115–17
Crossley family, 10
Crossley brothers, 41
Crossley, Mrs Edward, 37, 94
Crossley, Sir Francis, 14–15,
    51, 55, 116–17
Crossley, John (Sen), 108
Crossley, Martha, 108
Crossley Heath School, 35
Crossley Orphanage, 41–3
Crossley and Porter Orphan
    Home and School, 43
    Heath Grammar School,
        35–6, 44

Defoe, Daniel, 1, 3
Despard, Charlotte, 167
Divorce, 61–5, 95
    Matrimonial Causes Act
        (1857), 61–2
    Wife-selling, 62–3
        see also marriage
Dobson, Joseph, 120
Domestic chores *see*
    housework
Duffield, Margaret, 72, 78–9,
    100–101

Education Acts
    1869 Endowed Schools
        Act, 36

1870 Forster Education Act, 30
1902 Balfour Education Act, 31
1918 Fisher Education Act, 16–17, 32, 122
1921 Education Act, 32
1944 Education Act, 32
Elections
    1832 Reform Act, 140
    1867 Reform Act, 149
    1918 Representation of the People Act, 173
    1928 Equal Franchise Act, 173
    women canvassing, 89, 140, 148, 165–7
    women standing, 96–9
    women voting in:
        civic (council/municipal) elections, 133
        parliamentary elections, 133, 140–1, 155, 173–4
        school boards, 30
Elland Female Radical Association, 142–3
Engineering, women in 125–9
Equal Pay, 13, 61, 64–5, 108, 115
    clerks, 129–30
    Crossley's Carpets, 116–17
    Mackintosh's, 121
    teachers, 31
    textiles, 4–5, 97, 100, 114, 120
    engineering, 126–7

Family planning see birth control
    see also illegitimacy
    see also abortion
Fawcett, Millicent, 150, 163
Fielden, John, 9
Fisher-Smith, Lady, 84
Fitch, Joshua, 30, 32–5
Fundraising see voluntary work
Fustian weavers' strike, Hebden Bridge, 157–62, 170

Gawthorpe, Mary, 156–7, 160
Gledhill, Ian, 85–6
Goldthorpe, Leslie, 162

Half-timers, 32, 122
    see also mill schools
Halifax Building Society:
Hill, Sir Enoch, 134
    inception in 1853 (Old Cock Inn), 130–1
    Wilson, Kathleen (first female clerk), 131, 172
Halifax Citizens' Guild, 95–6
Halifax Council, 82, 96–7, 153–5
Halifax Council of Women Workers
    see voluntary work: National Council of Women
Halifax Girls' High School, 37–41, 49, 91

Halifax Girls' Secondary
    School, 40–1
Halifax Rural Deanery Moral
    Welfare Committee, 81–2
    see also Saint Margaret's
        House
Halifax School of Art, 47–8
Halifax Sunday School
    Union, 26
Halifax Technical College, 49,
    130–1
Halifax Working Men's
    College, 47
Halifax Young Women's
    Institute, 47
Health and Safety
    factories, 13, 123–5
    mines, 17–18, 20–4
    see also Silkstone Pit
        Disaster, Barnsley
Heath Grammar School see
    Crossley Heath School
Hebden Bridge Local History
    Society, 162
Heynemann, Dr, 84–5, 88
Hipperholme Grammar
    School, 35
Holdwsorth, John, 3, 11–12,
    113
    see also Shaw Lodge Mills
Horner, Charles, 122–3
Housework, 51–8, 107
    Bentley, Phyllis, 38–9, 49,
        56, 92
Humphreys, Rita, 43–4, 68,
    79–80, 107, 109–11

Illegitimacy, 77, 79–82, 104–
    105
    see also birth control
    see also Saint Margaret's
        House
Independent Labour Party
    (ILP), 152, 160, 166–7
Infanticide, 77–8, 142

Jones, Ernest, 148–9
Jones, Dr Helena, 171–2
Joseph Sykes Brothers, 3–4, 6

Kenney, Annie, 153, 155
Kershaw, Patience, 21–4

Latchmore, Dr Alice, 73–6, 85
Lightowler, Miriam, 86–7,
    96–7
Lister, Anne, 59, 61, 63, 66–7,
    90–1
    colliery/mine-owner, 22–3
    domestic servants, 105–
        106, 110
    education, 29, 34, 46, 89
    politics, 139, 140–1
Lord Nelson Inn, Luddenden,
    4
Lowell Textile Mills, 13

Mackintosh, Harold, 121
Mackintosh, John, 120–2, 129
Mackintosh, Violet, 120
Marriage, 39, 59–65
    Financial reasons for, 61,
        89–90, 92

Infant Custody Act
(1873), 60
Leaving work on, 61, 65, 110,
103–104, 114–15, 135

Married Women's Property
Acts 1870 and 1872, 60
Maternal mortality, 71–2, 74,
77, 86
Maternity and Child Welfare
Centre, Northgate, 74, 85,
87
Mechanics' Institute, 47,
149–50, 171
Mill schools, 29
Mines and Collieries
Regulation Act (1842),
23–4
Mines, Children's
Employment Commission
into (1842), 17–18
Mount Zion Sunday School,
26–7
Munition work *see* war work
Murgatroyd, Reverend John,
104

National Birth Control
Association, 84
National Council of Women
(NCW) *see* Voluntary
work
National Society of Women's
Suffrage, 149
National Union of Women's
Suffrage Societies
(NUWSS), 150, 165

Northgate Hotel, 19
Northgate End Chapel, 34,
47, 56, 64

Oastler, Richard, 10–12, 14,
110
'Slavery in Yorkshire'
letter, *Leeds Mercury*,
6–9
Statue, 17
York 'Pilgrimage of
Mercy', 15–16
Oddfellows' Hall, 15, 139
Old Cock Inn, 10, 100, 130
Old Lane Mill, 12, 114
Ovenden Senior School, 44–5

Pankhurst, Adela, 160
Pankhurst, Emmeline, 160,
162, 165–8, 170–1
Parry, Captain William,
59–60
People's Charter, the, 141–2
Peterloo massacre, 139–40
Philip, John Birnie, 17
Piece Hall, 26
Plug riots, 144–9
Poverty, 52, 73–5, 77, 86,
144–5
see also welfare
Pregnancy, 60, 73, 77–8, 104
death in childbirth *see*
maternal mortality
Priestley, Edward, 46
Priestley, J.B., 70–1
Princess Mary's School, 40–1
Prostitution, 77, 111

Quakers, 30, 103
Queenshead (Queensbury)
    school and church, 94

Ranger, William:
Report on Sanitary
    Conditions in Halifax
    (1851), 52
Rawson, Jeremiah, 23
Rawson family, 10
Rawson governess (Miss
    King), 33
Rawson mine (Swan Bank),
    19–20, 23
Reach, Angus Béthune,
    112–14
Representation of the People
    Act (1918) see Elections
Riley's Toffee Works, 121
Rishworth Grammar School,
    35
Roe, Dr, 83, 85–7
Roomfield Baptist Church, 26

Sadler, Michael see Sadler
    Report
Sadler Report (Report of
    the Select Committee on
    Factory Children's Labour
    1831-2), 11–12, 14
Saint Augustine's Girls'
    School, 32
Saint Margaret's House, 80–4
Saltonstall, Lavena, 60, 156,
    162, 174
    census (1911), 171

fustian weavers' strike,
    157–8
imprisonment, 165–6,
    169–70
Women's Labour League,
    152–4
School Board, Halifax, 30–1,
    37
School-leaving age, 32
    see also half-timers
Schools' Inquiry Commission
    (1868), 29–30, 32–7, 41,
    45, 47
Scott, D.M., 40
Shibden Hall, 22, 91, 140–1
    domestic servants, 105–
    107
Silkstone Pit Disaster,
    Barnsley, 18–19, 23
Scriven, Samuel, 19–22
Sex Disqualification
    (Removal) Act (1919), 101
Shaw Lodge Mills, 12, 112–14
Smith, Barker and Willson,
    126–8
Smith, James
    Report on the Condition
        of the Town of
        Halifax (1845), 52–3
Social Security see Welfare
Standing Conference of
    Women's Organisations
    (SCWO) see Voluntary
    work
Steedman, Carolyn, 104
Stocks, Joseph, 19–20, 22
Sunday School Jubilees, 26

'Surplus women', 91–2, 131
Sykes, Walter, 6

Taylor, Mary, 152, 154, 156–7, 167
   census (1911), 171–2
   fustian weavers' strike, 158–9
   imprisonment, 163–5, 174
Ten Hour Bill, 13, 17–18, 151
   Factory Act (1847), 16
      see also Oastler, Richard
      see also Sadler Report
Tramworkers' strike, 152–6, 158–9, 170

Voluntary work, 14, 44, 94–9, 109
   Anti-Corn Law League, 14–15
   anti-slavery movement, 30
   Beacon Club, the, 98
   Blakey, Esther, 30
   fundraising:
   Bazaars, 94
   Saint Margaret's House, 81
   National Council of Women (NCW), 96–9
   Standing Conference of Women's Organisations (SCWO), 98–9
   Temperance movement, 30
      see also Band of Hope

Women's Voluntary Service (WVS), 99
   see also Yorkshire Ladies Council of Education
Votes for Women see Elections
Voting see Elections

Walker, Selwyn, 3–4
War work, 56–8, 65, 93, 99, 101–102, 122, 173
   clerks, 130–3, 135
   munitions, 91, 127
   women in engineering, 125–7
   women in textile mills, 117, 119
Welfare, 102
   Halifax Council of Social Welfare, 96
   Poor Laws, 96, 141–3
   poor relief, 141–2
Welfare State, 109
Wife-selling see Divorce
Whitehall Hotel Hipperholme, 4
Whitley, Mrs Nathan, 31, 37, 94
Wilson, Benjamin, 139–41, 148
Wilson, Kathleen see Halifax Building Society; Wilson, Kathleen
Willson, Laura Annie, 129–30
   census (1911), 171, 174
   house building, 128–9
   engineering, 126–8

fustian weavers' strike,
    157–60, 162
imprisonment, 160–2,
    165–6, 168
Women's Labour League, 152,
    166–7
women's suffrage, 156–7,
    167–71
Women's Engineering Society,
    127–8, 174
Women's Freedom League,
    167–8
Women's Labour League,
    152–6, 166–7
Women's Social and Political
    Union (WSPU), 150–1,
    156–7, 161–71, 173–4

census (1911), 171–2
    see also fustian weavers'
        strike, Hebden Bridge
    see also tramworkers'
        strike
Women's Welfare Clinic, 84–8
Wordsworth, Dorothy, 34
Working hours, 4, 8–9, 11,
    16–17, 151
    see also Ten Hour Bill

Yorkshire Ladies Council of
    Education, 37, 94